Egon Schiele:
154 Drawings and Watercolors

By Narim Bender

First Edition

*****

I0464836

Egon Schiele: 154 Drawings and Watercolors
*****

Foreword

Egon Schiele (1890 - 1918) was an Austrian painter, a protégé of Gustav Klimt and important figurative painter of the early 20th century. The twisted body shapes and the expressive line that characterize his paintings and drawings mark the artist as one an earliest exponent of Expressionism. In Schiele's early years, he was strongly influenced by Klimt and Kokoschka but soon evolved into his own characteristic style. Some critics view Schiele's work as being grotesque, erotic, pornographic, or disturbing, focusing on sex, death, and discovery. Shiele answered to them in that way:

"To restrict the artist is a crime. It is to murder germinating life".

He was born in 1890 in Lower Austria as the third child in his family. His father was a rail-road civil servant who died in 1905. His uncle became his protector but did not support his artistic career. Nevertheless, Schiele entered the academy in Vienna where he quickly ran into difficulties with his teacher, the then famous Professor Griepenkerl.

In 1907 he met Gustav Klimt, whom he admired, who assisted him in obtaining his first commissions and who influenced his early drawing style. Following Klimt's suggestion, Schiele entered four paintings in the Vienna International Exhibition of 1909, where works by Oskar Kokoschka and Vincent Van Gogh were also shown. In the same year he left the academy and, with other young artists, formed the short-lived artist group "Neukunstgruppe"; however, the first exhibition was not successful. By 1910 he had found his own style with its strong emphasis on the contour line and vibrant colors.

In 1911 he moved to the small town of Krumau, where he painted a number of townscapes. His lifestyle caused problems in the town and he moved with his model Wally Neuziel to Neulengbach where in 1912 he was arrested and charged with immorality and seduction. Some of his drawings were confiscated; one was even burned by the judge in the courtroom. He spent 24 traumatic days in jail and returned to Vienna upon his release.

His first important exhibitions were held in Germany: in 1913 in the famous Galerie Goltz in Munich and in the Folkwangmuseum in Hagen, followed by one-man exhibits in Hamburg, Breslau, Stuttgart, and Berlin, where the Expressionist journal Die Aktion published his drawings as well as his poetry. In 1915 he married Edith Harms, and a few days later he was drafted into the army. After having been assigned to guard Russian prisoners of war, the Die Aktion journal published a special issue with his drawings and the Berlin Sezession exhibited his works.

In 1917 he was transferred to the Army Museum in Vienna, which provided him with some time to paint again. A portfolio of 12 drawing reproductions was published. He was invited to participate in exhibits in Munich, Dresden, Amsterdam, and Stockholm, but his poverty remained unchanged. The first truly great success came in 1918 with his exhibit at the Vienna Secession (no less than 19 paintings and several drawings). He received a number of commissions, and 25 of his works were exhibited in Zurich. Shortly thereafter, however, his wife—who was expecting a child-died of the Spanish influenza epidemic, and three days later the artist succumbed to the same disease.

Schiele's dominating theme was the human body, which he depicts in truly singular forms. Likewise in his paintings of children he emphasized their awkward bodies and their earnest eyes, and yet, the impact of these works on the viewer is very strong because the depictions are forthright and direct. Even his marvelous townscapes frequently lack perspective dimensions and let the windows of the houses appear like blind eyes; they are expressions of the artist's mood more than topographical depictions; they are images of fall—with isolated, dry trees standing in the cold wind.

Schiele's symbolic works, such as "Death and the Maiden," "The Hermits," or even such seemingly happy themes as "Mother with Two Children," show the same penetrating insight for which his portraits have become famous. His many self-portraits are proof of his continuous struggle with what he considered the soul of the arts: the depiction of that truth which lies below the surface. While the subject matter seems to be depressing, his works prove otherwise. The extraordinary ability to form the three dimensional body through dominating contour lines, his choice of very strong and forthright colors, the frequently ambiguous spaces, and his extraordinary sensitivity, which transforms even a seemingly quick drawing into a complete work of art, have allowed Schiele's fame to continue to grow.

He focused on portraits of others as well as himself. In his later years, while he still worked often with nudes, they were done in a more realist fashion. Schiele made many drawings, some of which were extremely erotic. During his short but highly prolific career which ended with his premature death, Schiele created more than three thousand works on paper and approximately three hundred paintings.

With his signature graphic style, embrace of figural distortion, and bold defiance of conventional norms of beauty, Egon Schiele was one of the leading figures of Austrian Expressionism.

Drawings and Watercolors

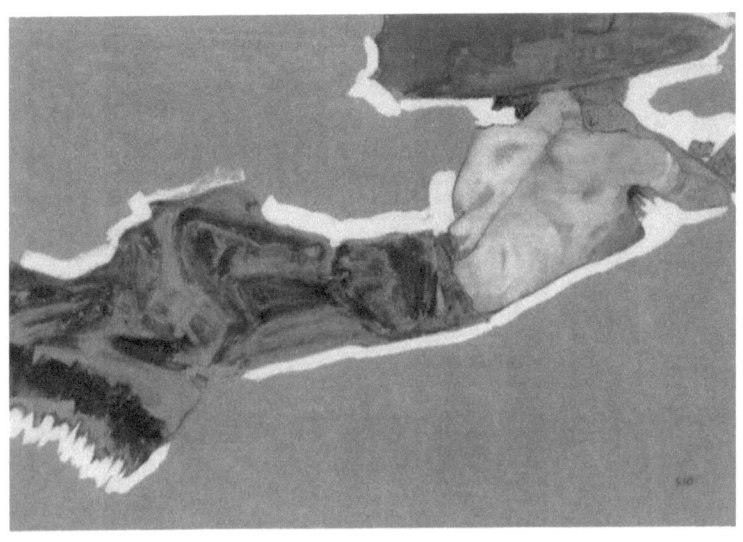

Reclining Semi-Nude with Red Hat

1910, Gouache, watercolor and crayon with white heightening, Private collection

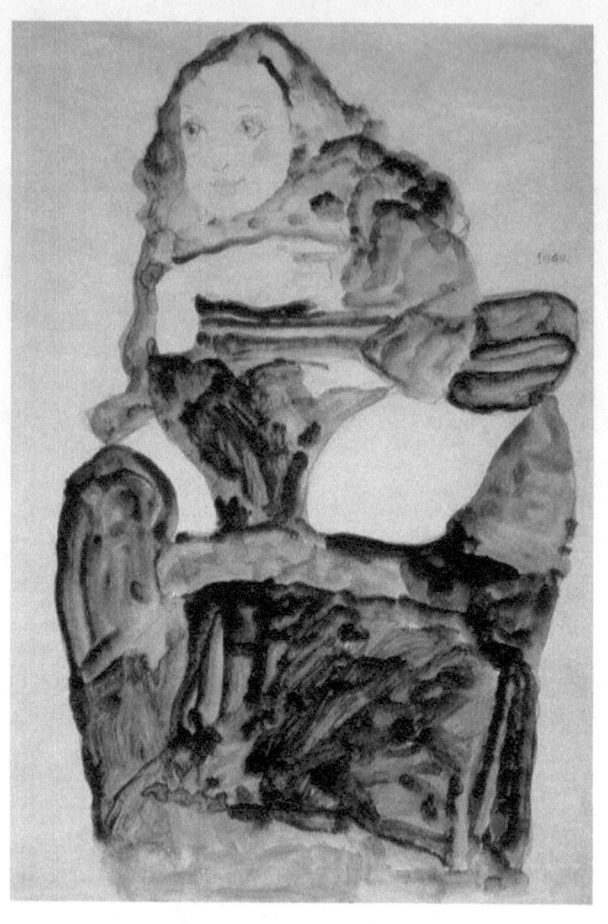

Seated Girl with Raised Left Leg

1911, Gouache, watercolor and pencil on paper, Private collection

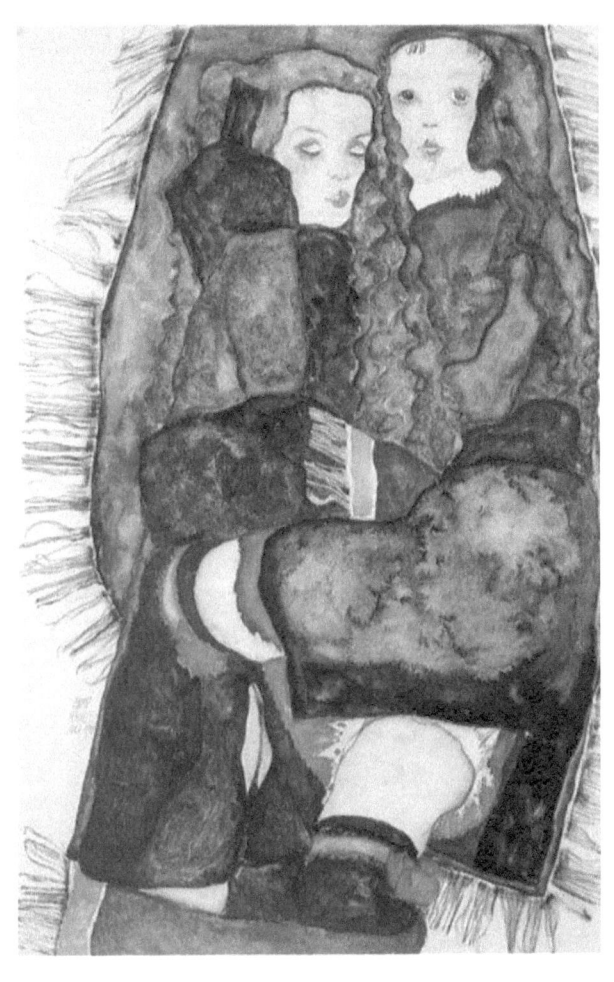

Two Girls on a Fringed Blanket

1911, Gouache, watercolor and pencil on paper, 55.9 cm x 36.8 cm, Private collection

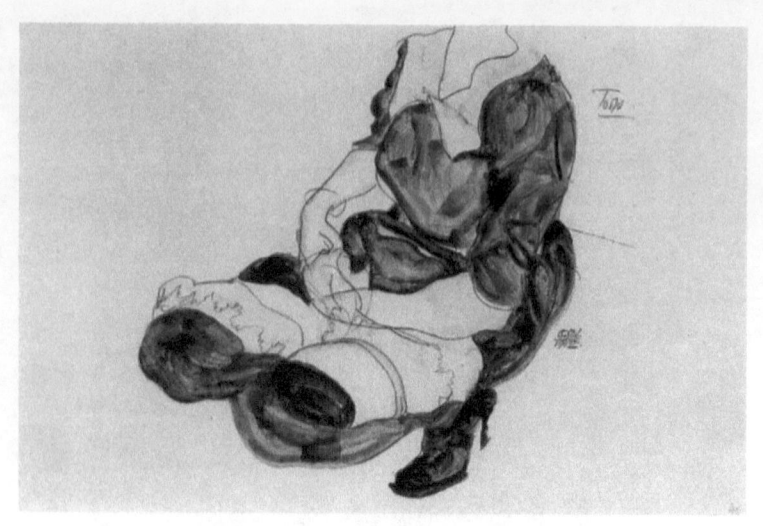

Female Torso, Squatting

1912, Watercolor and pencil on paper, Private collection

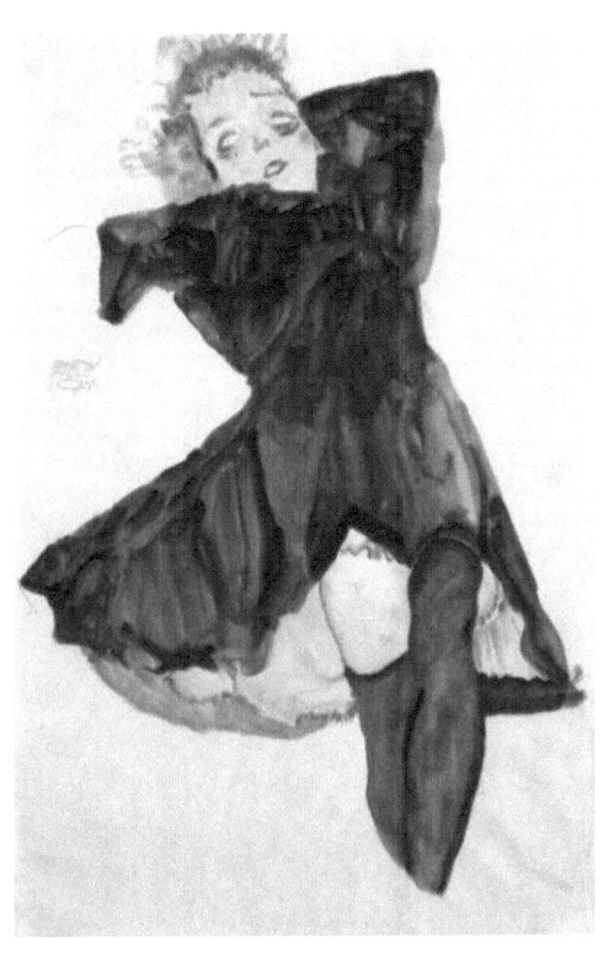

Girl in Blue Dress

1911, watercolor and pencil on paper, 47.8 x 31.7 cm,
Private collection

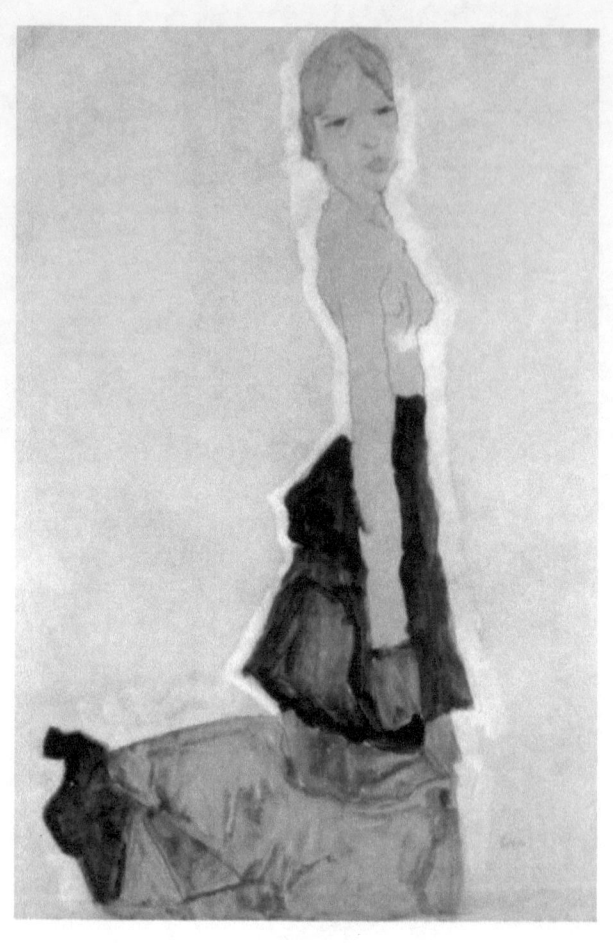

Kneeling Semi-Nude

1911, Gouache, watercolor, pencil and white heightening on paper, Private collection

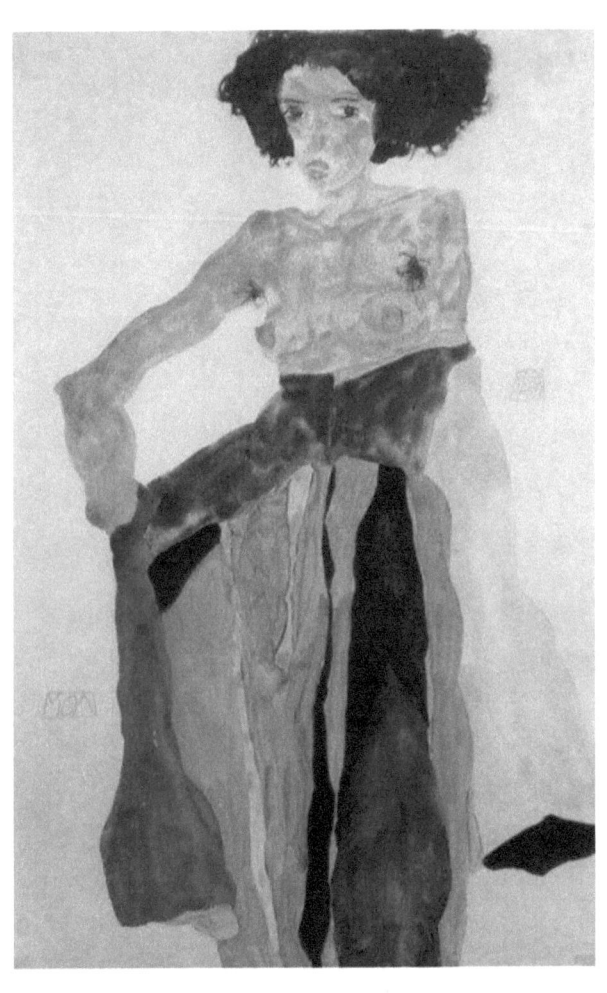

Moa

1911, Gouache, watercolor and pencil on paper, Private collection

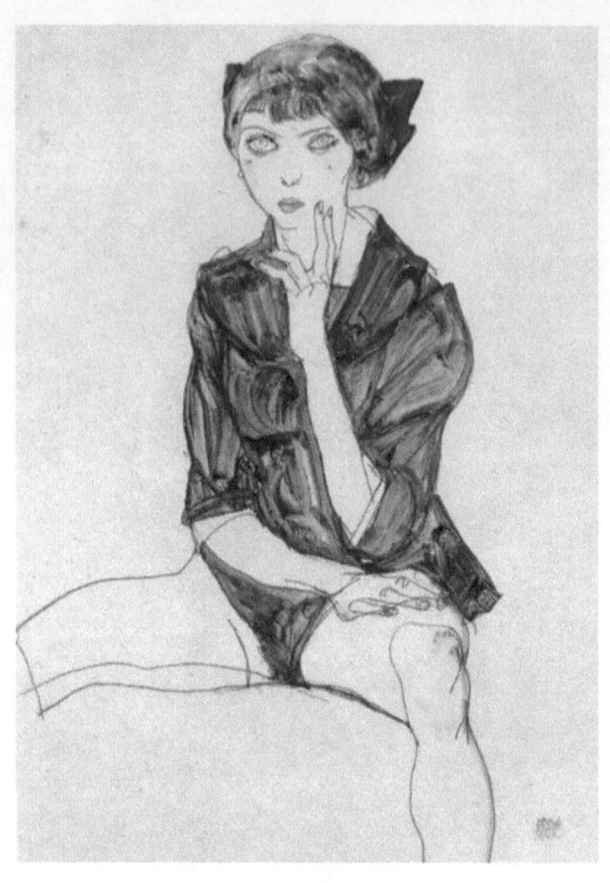

Sitting Woman in a Green Blouse

1913, Gouache, watercolor and pencil on paper, Private collection

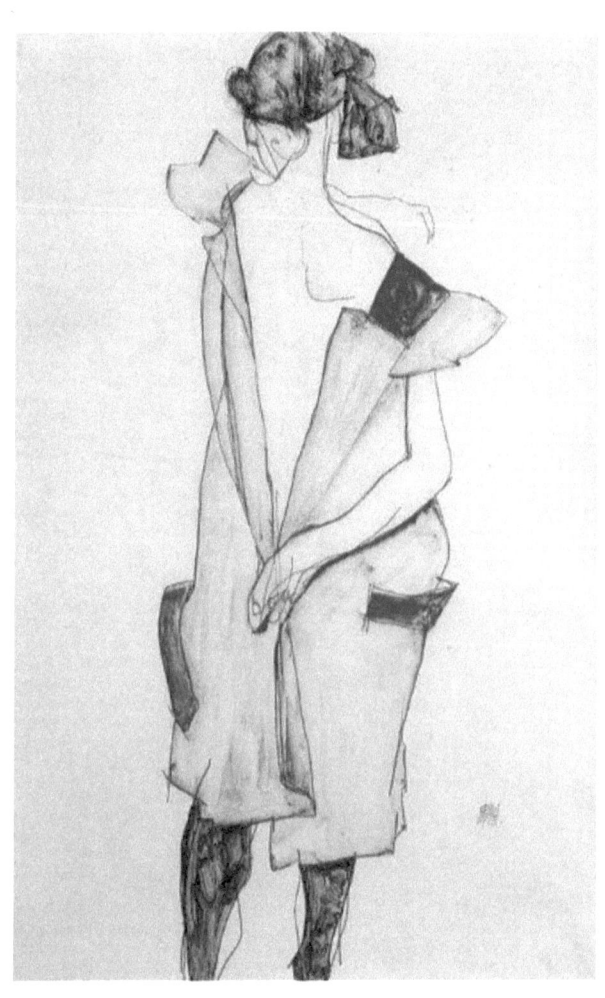

Standing Girl in a Blue Dress and Green Stockings, Back View

1913, Watercolor and pencil on paper, Private collection

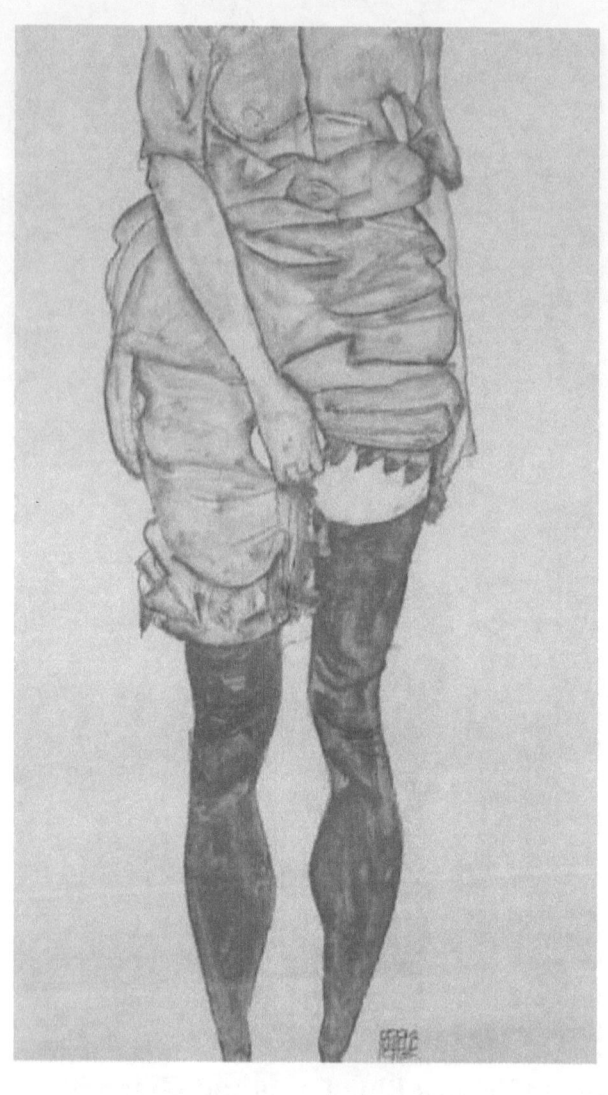

Standing Woman in Red

1913, Gouache, watercolor and pencil, Private collection

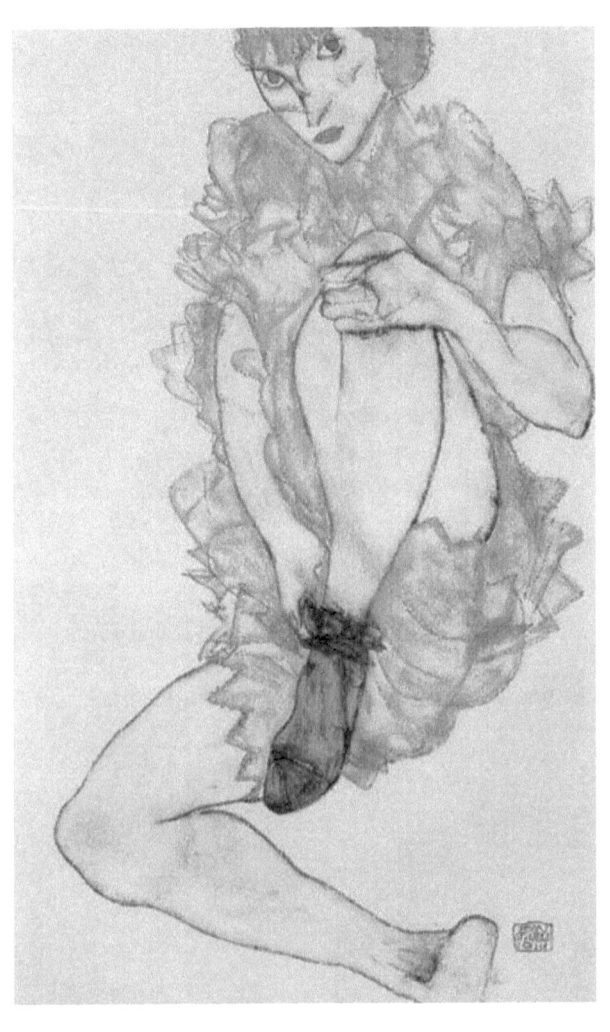

The Green Stocking

1914, Gouache and pencil on paper, Private collection

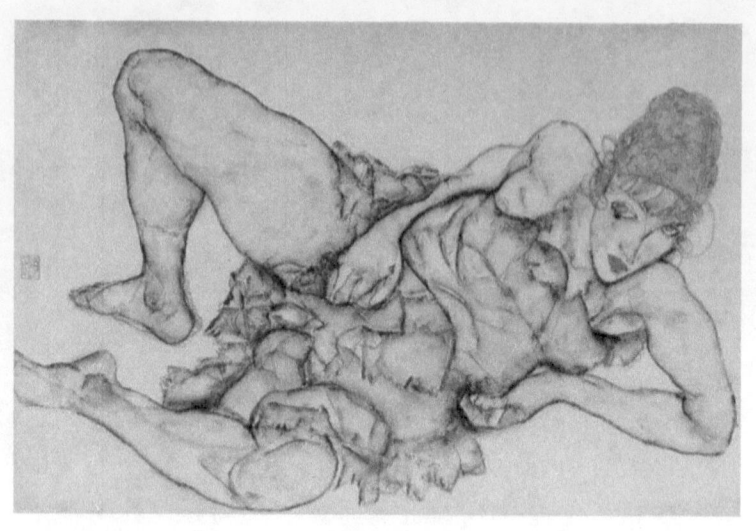

Reclining Woman with Blond Hair

1914, Gouache, watercolor and pencil on paper, Baltimore Museum of Art

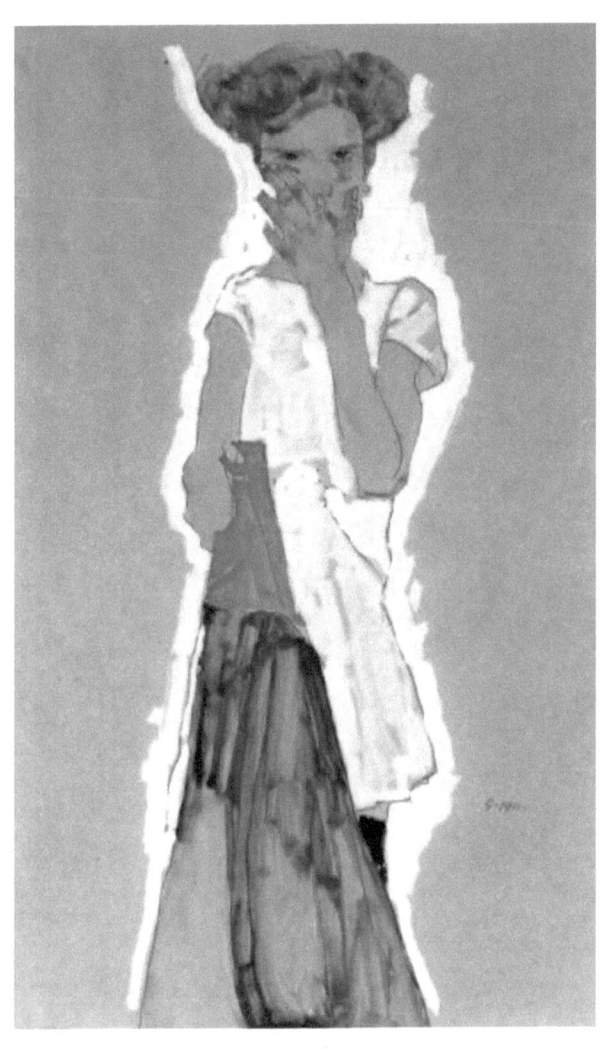

Standing Girl in White Underwear

1911, Gouache, watercolor and pencil on paper, Private collection

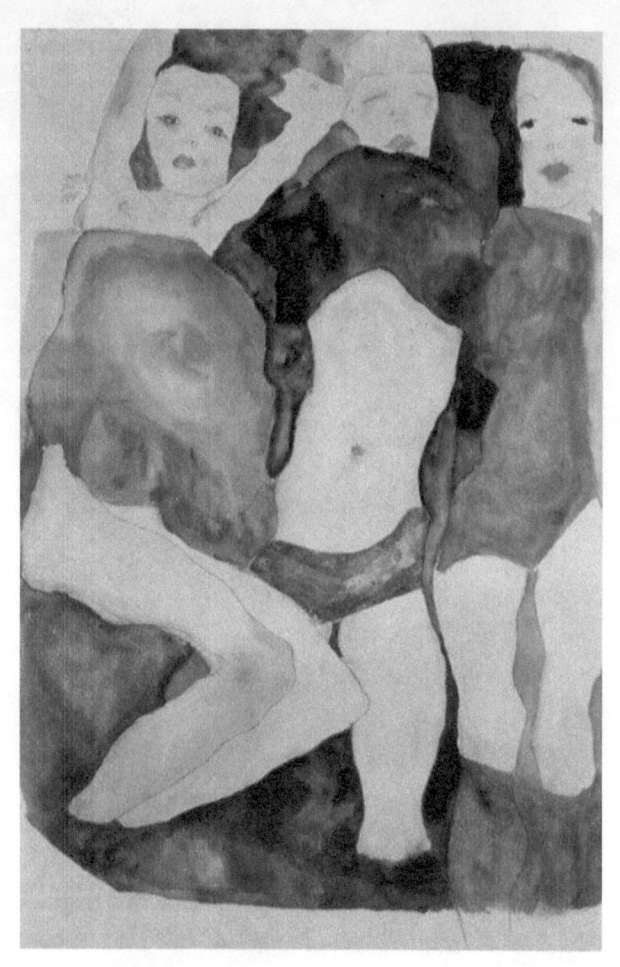

Three Girls

1911, Watercolor, Private collection

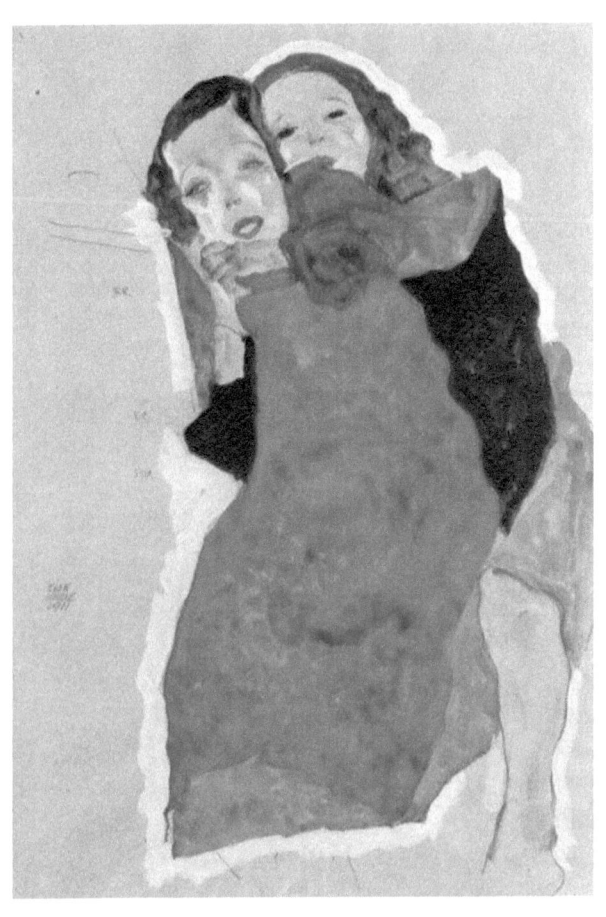

Two Girls

*1911, Pencil, watercolor, gouache and white body color,
Private collection*

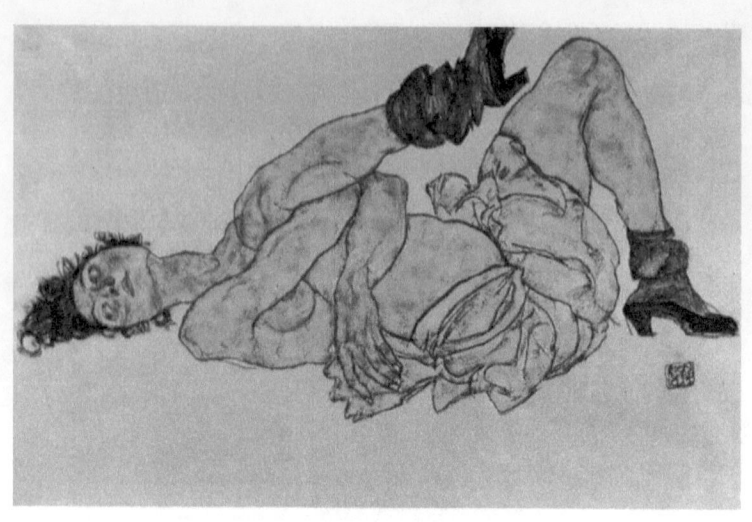

Reclining Female Nude

1917, Gouache, watercolor and charcoal, Private collection

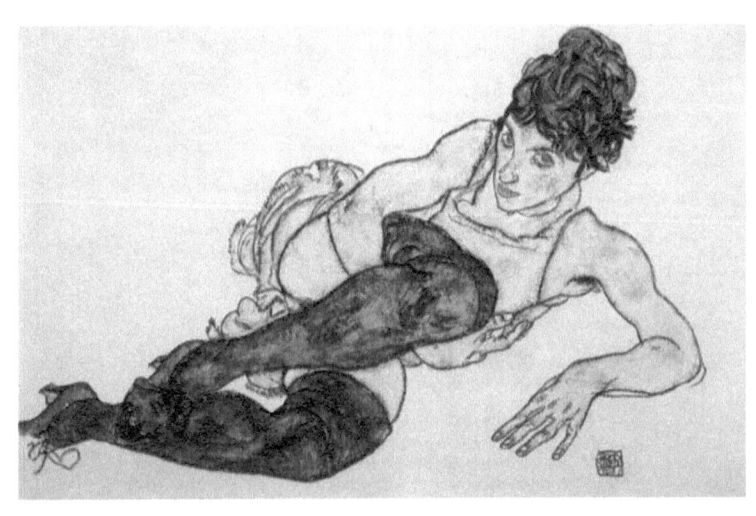

Reclining Woman with Green Stockings

1917, Gouache and black crayon on paper, Private collection

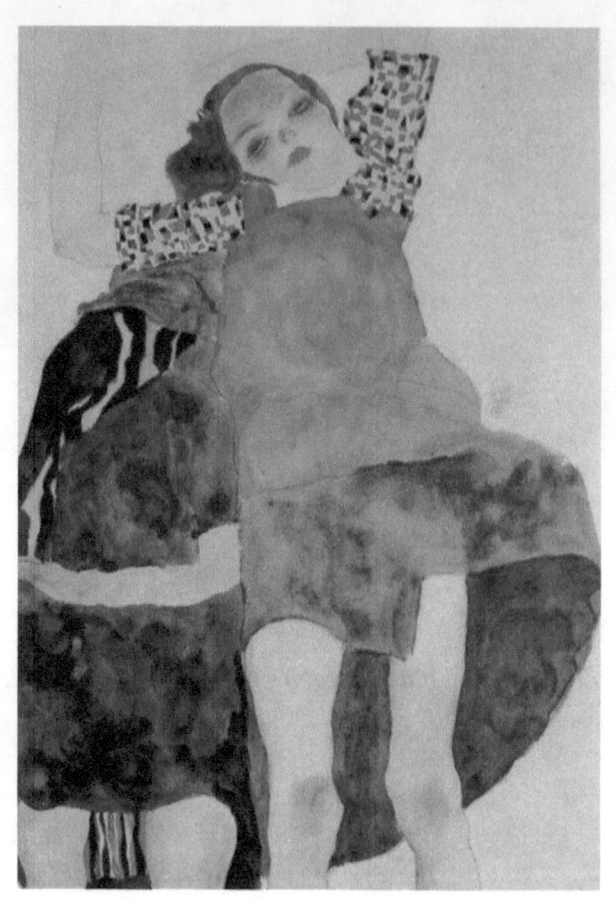

Two Seated Girls

1911, Watercolor, Private collection

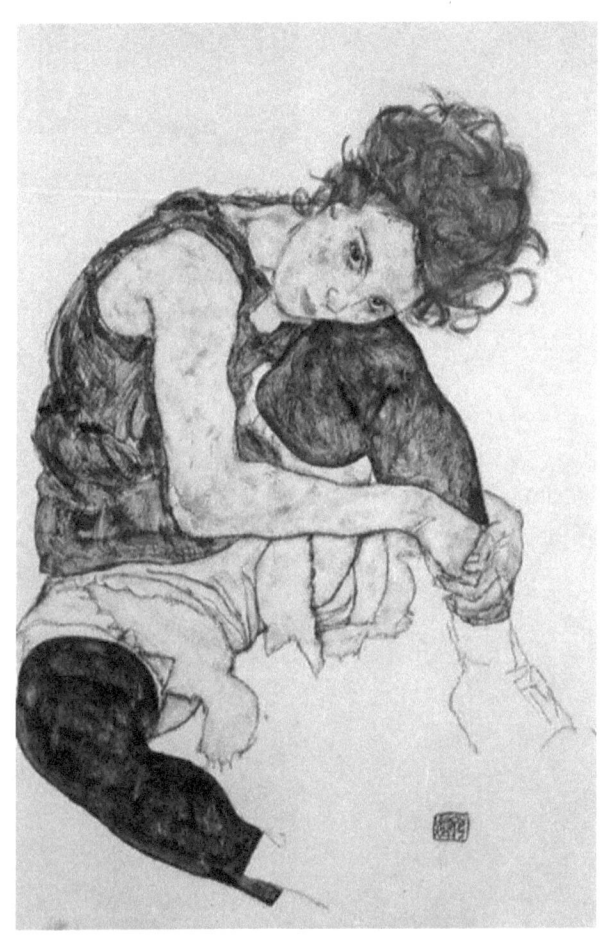

Seated Woman with Bent Knee

1917, Gouache, watercolor and pencil on paper, National Gallery - Prague

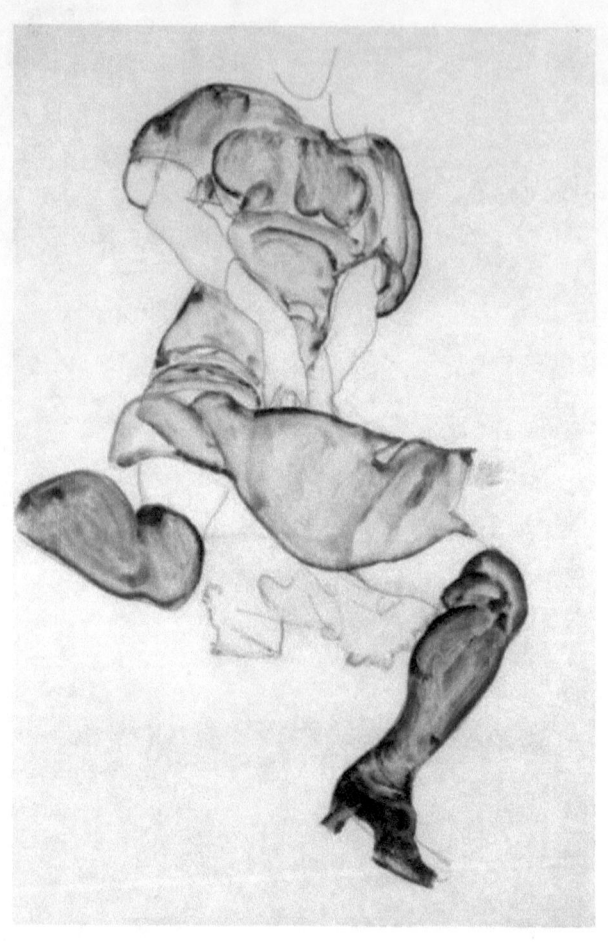

Woman with Black Stockings

1912, Watercolor and pencil on paper, Private collection

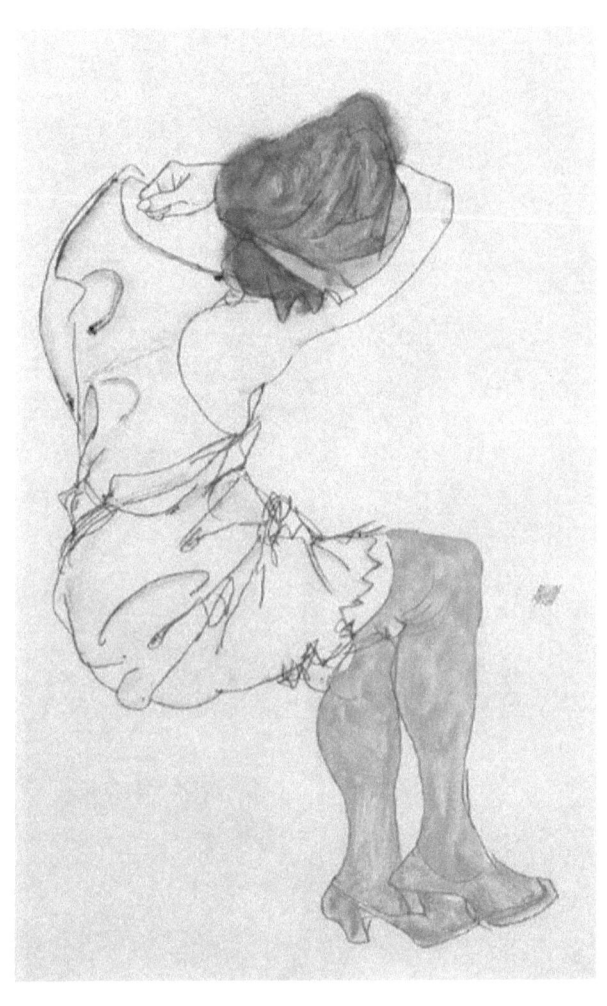

The Sleeping Girl

1913, Gouache, watercolor and pencil on paper, Private collection

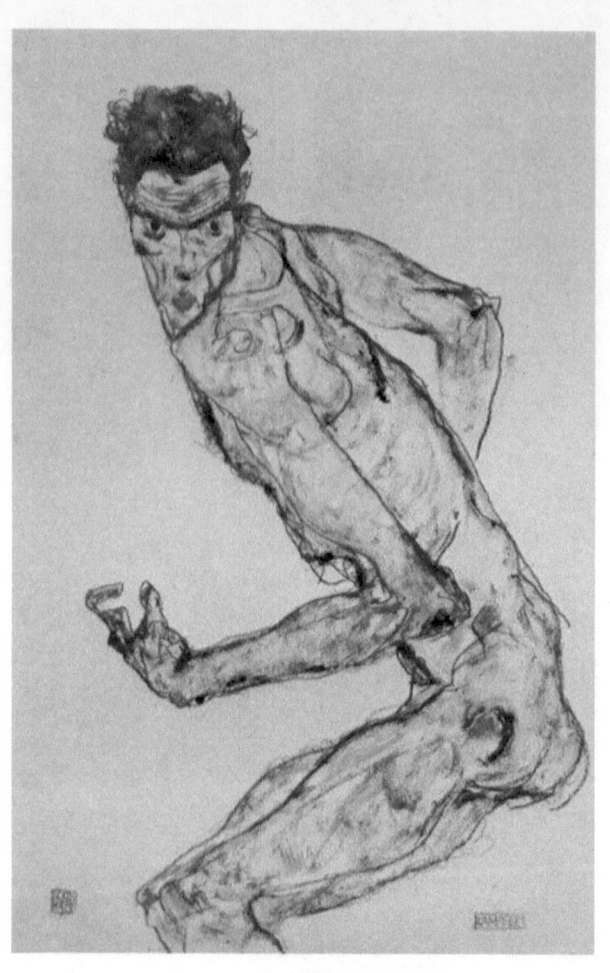

Fighter

1913, Pencil and gouache on paper, Private collection

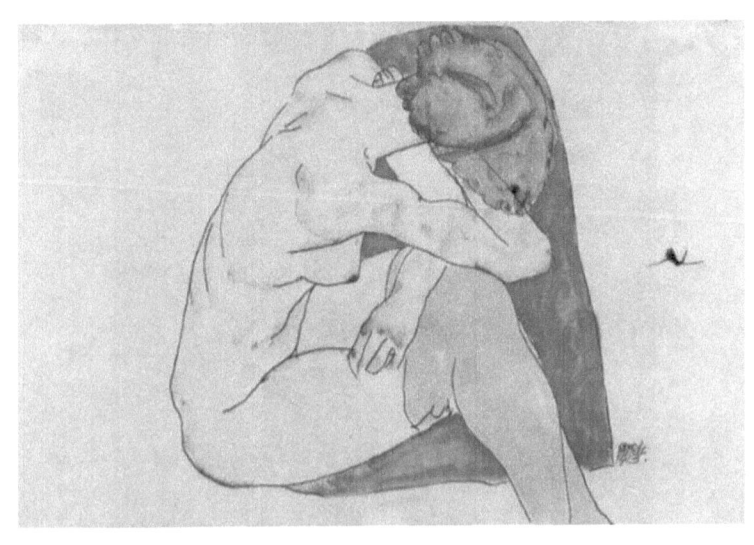

Seated Woman

*1913, Watercolor and black crayon on paper, Private
collection*

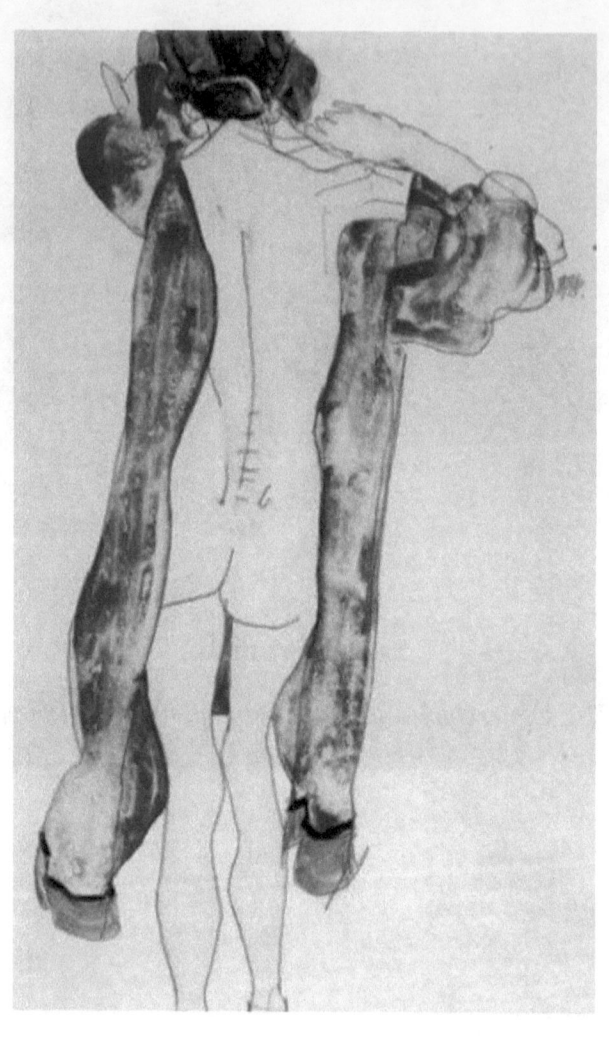

Standing Female Nude in a Blue Robe

1913, Pencil and gouache on paper, Private collection

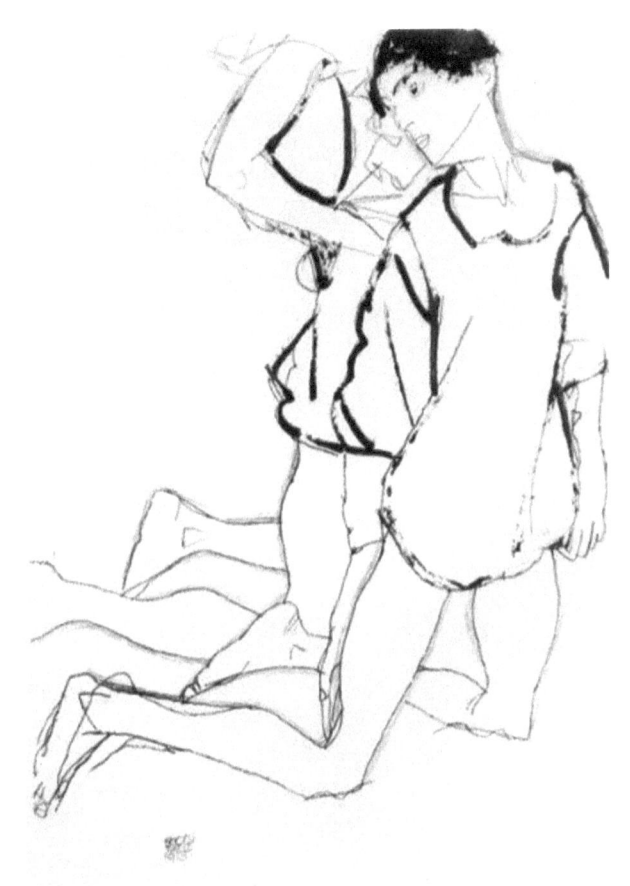

Two Kneeling Figures

1913, Pencil and India ink on paper, Private collection

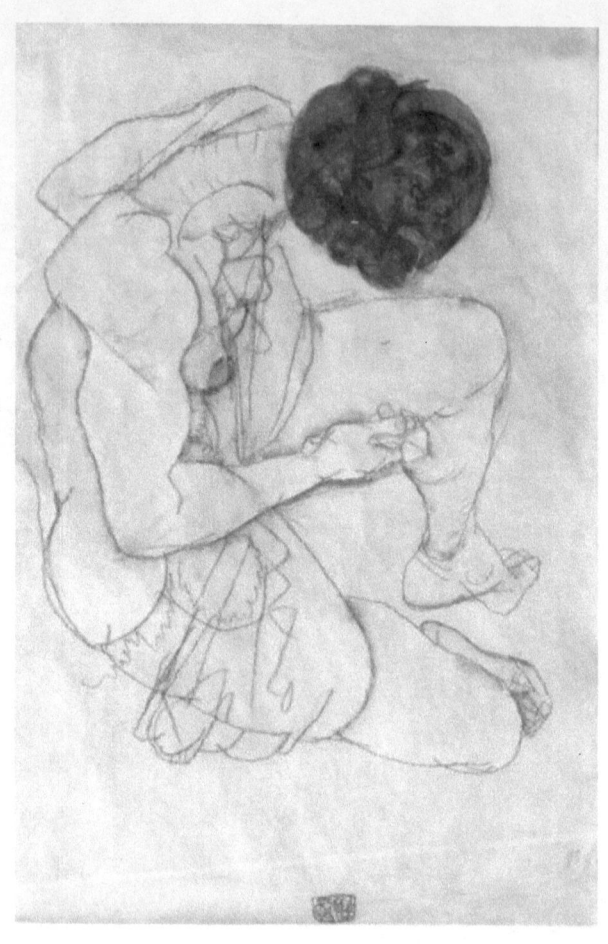

Sitting Woman

1914, Gouache and pencil on paper, Private collection

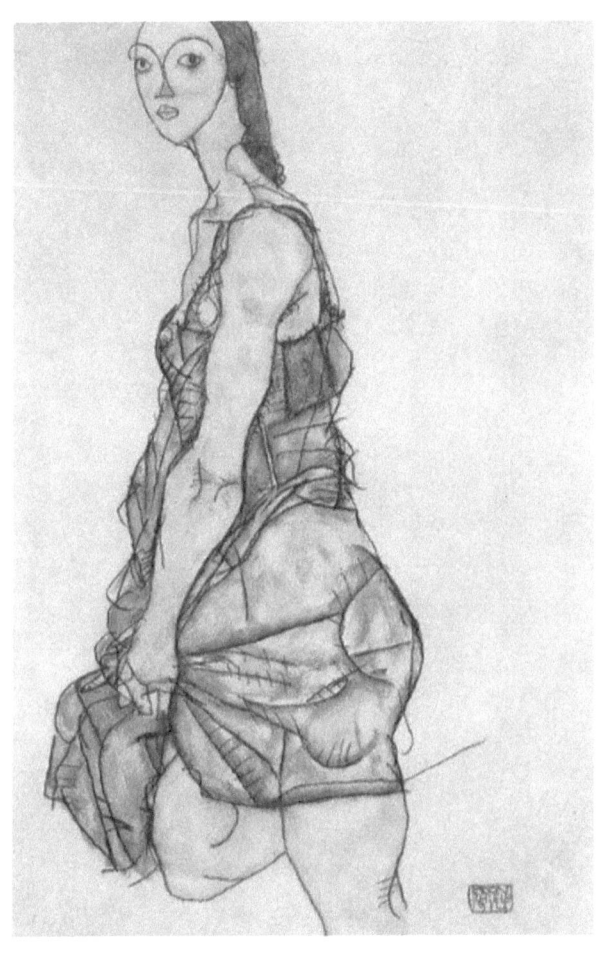

Standing Woman in a Green Skirt

1914, Gouache, watercolor and pencil on paper, Private collection

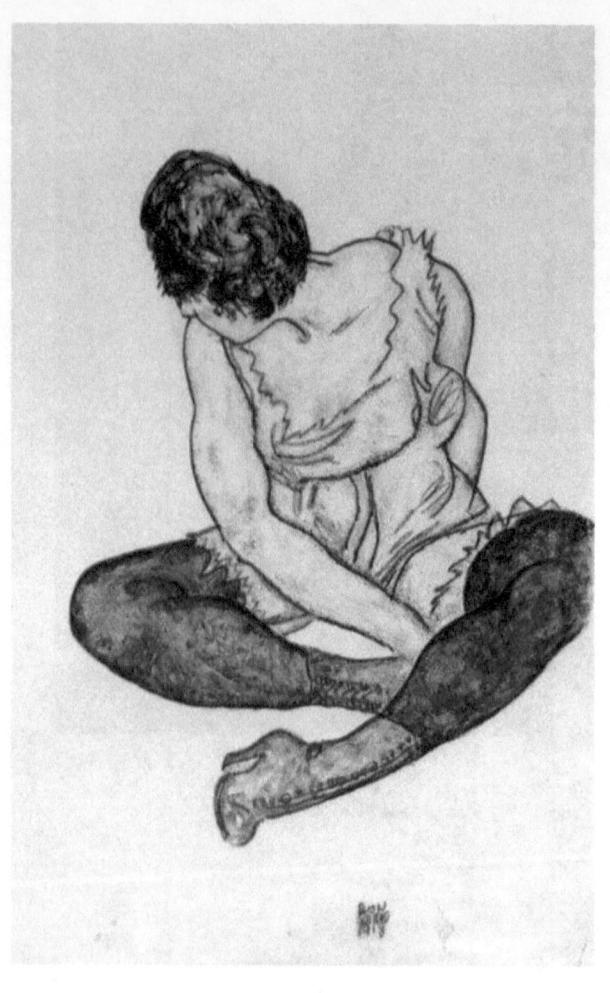

Seated Woman with Green Stockings

1918, Watercolor, gouache and pencil on buff paper, Private collection

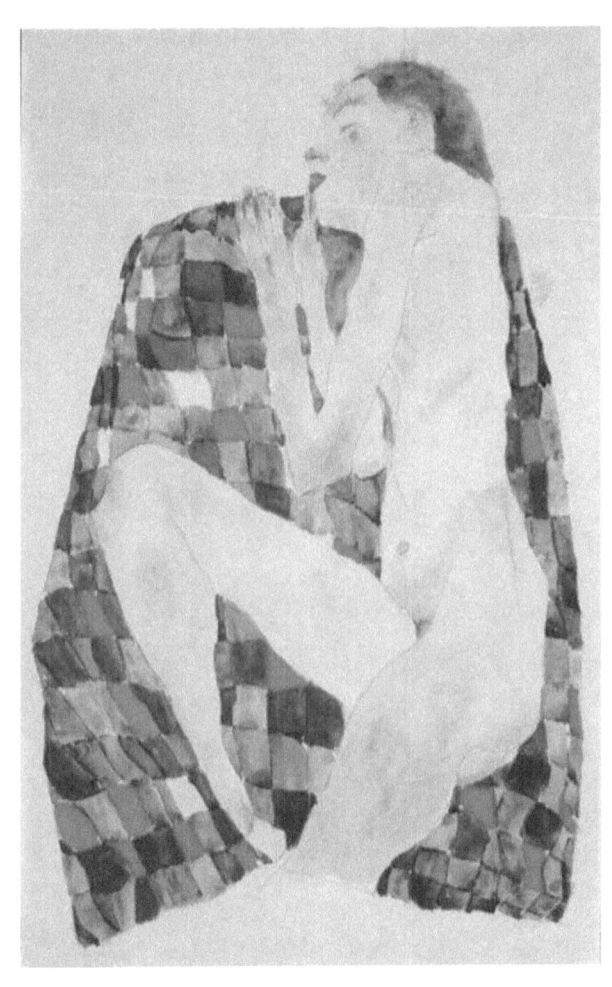

Female Nude

1911, Pencil, watercolor, Neue Galerie Graz

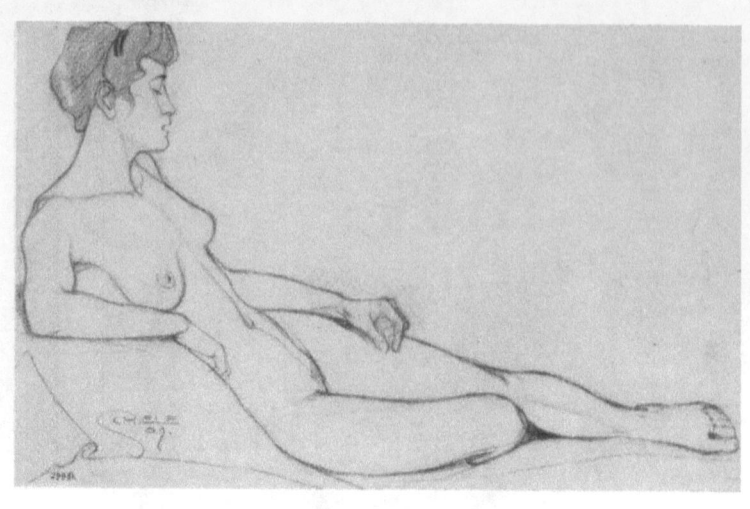

Lying woman

1908, pencil and chalk on paper (blue-gray), Albertina

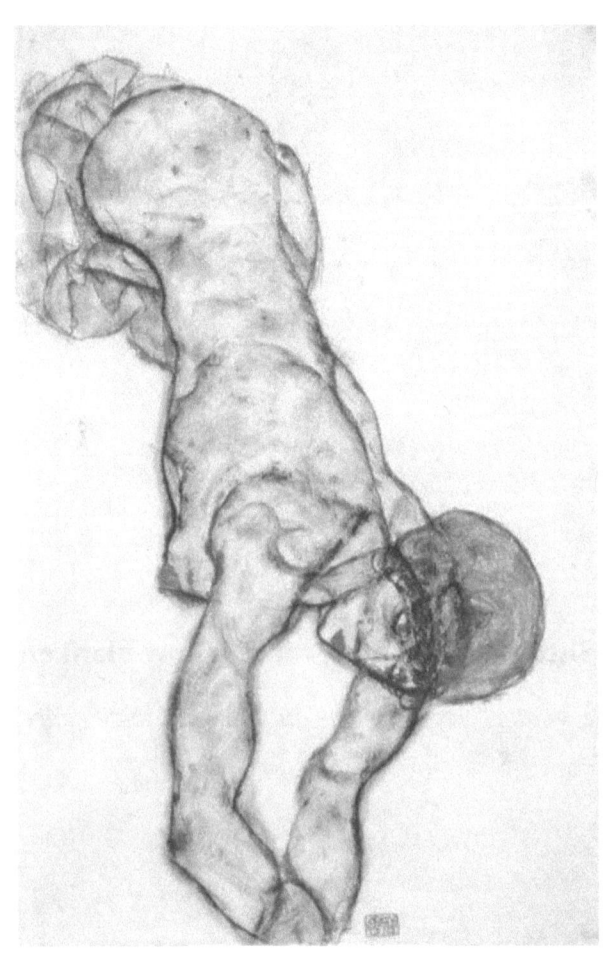

Nude with green hood

1914, Watercolor, gouache on paper, Albertina

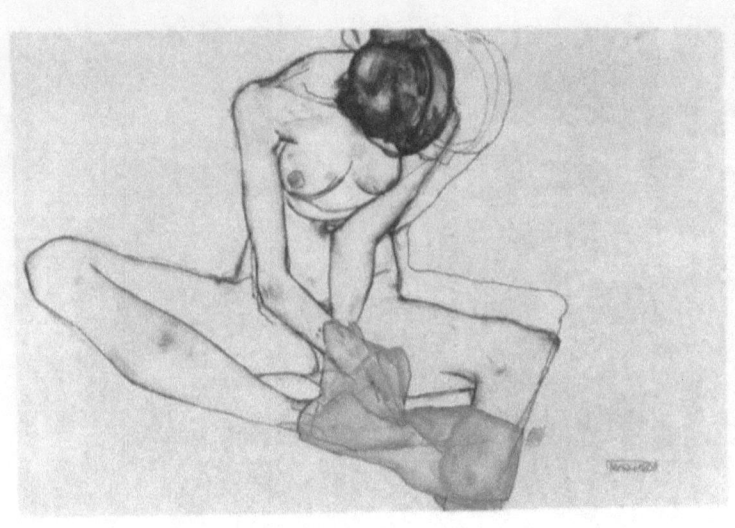

Sitting female nude with yellow blankett

1910, Watercolor, gouache on paper, Private collection

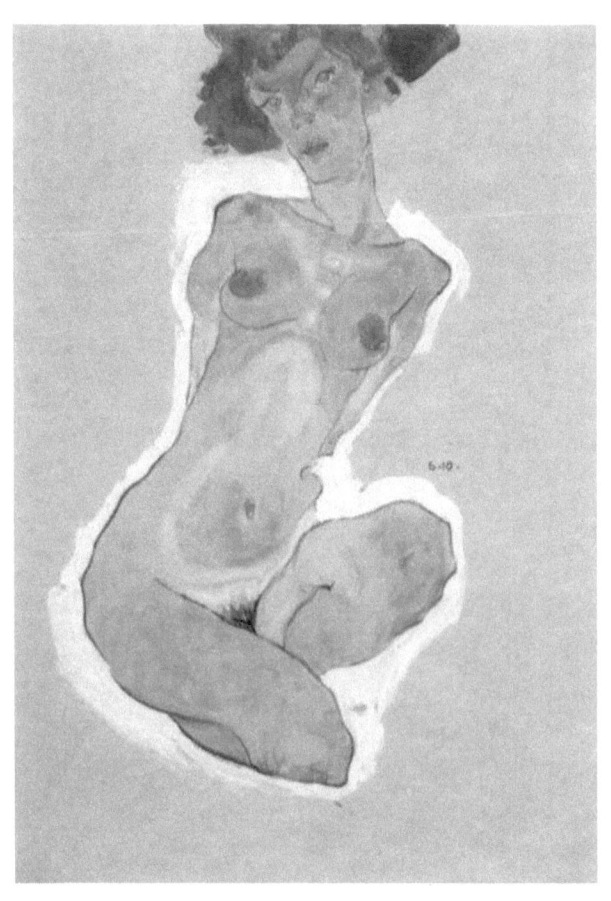

Crouching female nude

1910, chalk, body color on paper, Leopold Collection, Vienna

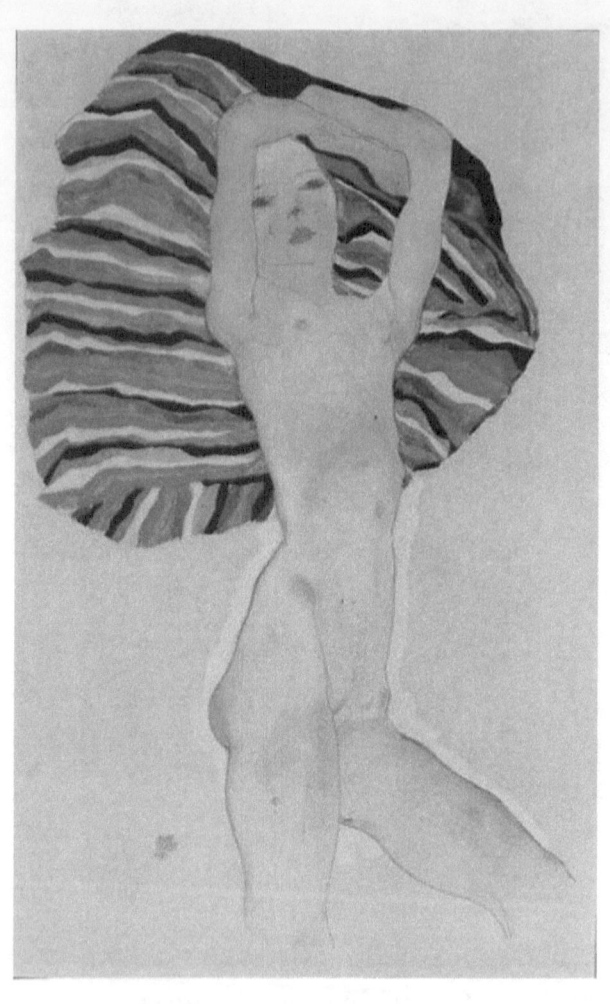

Girl act against colored cloth

1911, Pencil and gouache with watercolor on paper, Public collection

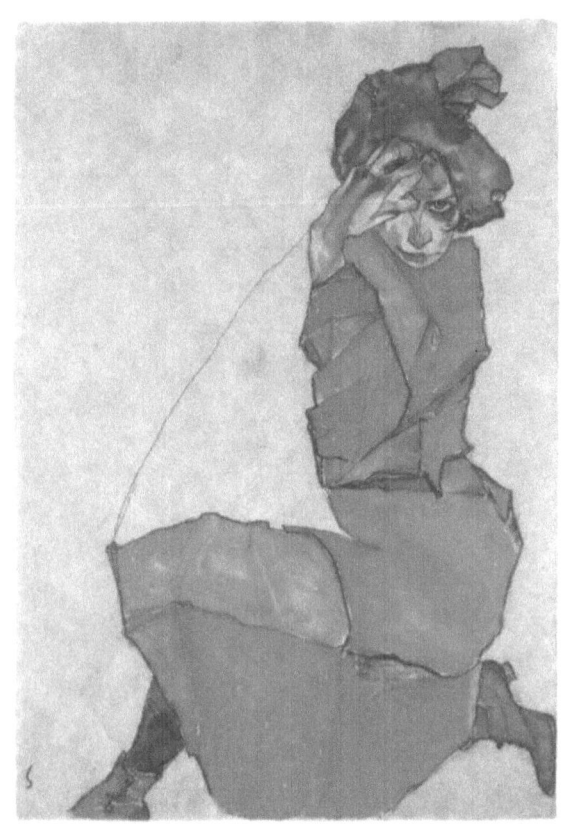

Kneeling girl with red-orange cloth

Date Unknown, Pencil and gouache with watercolor on paper, Private collection

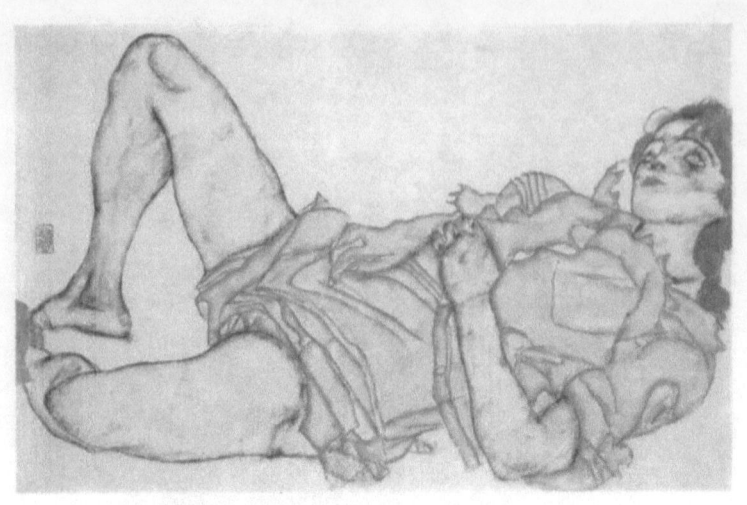

Lying woman with yellow dress

1914, watercolor, gouache on paper, Private collection

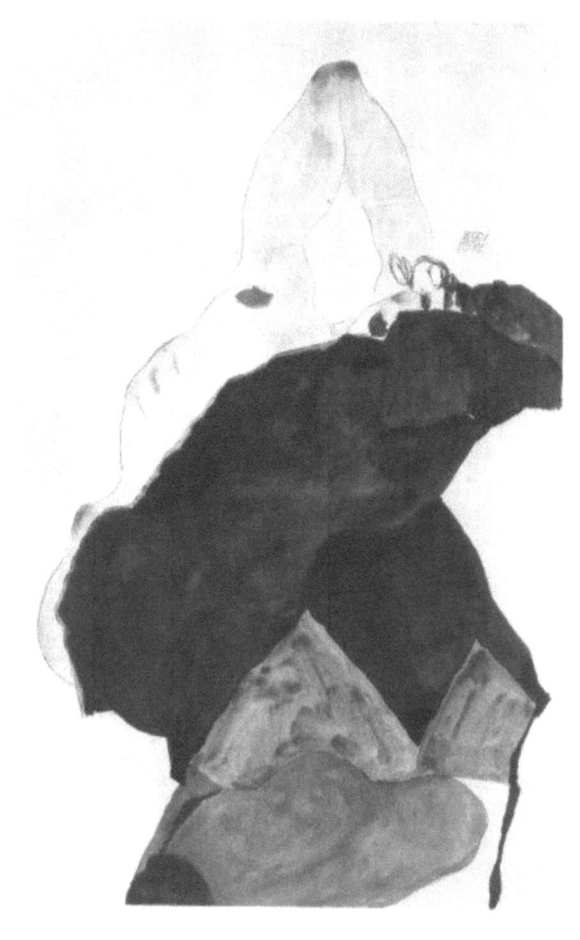

Girl with raised elbow

1911, watercolor, gouache on paper, Private collection

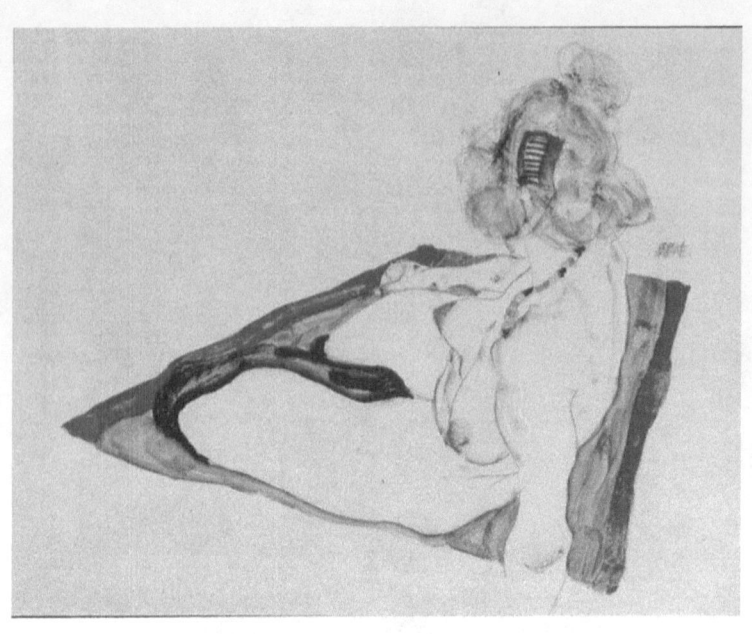

Blonde nude model sitting on brown cloth

*1912, watercolor, gouache, pencil on paper, 32 x 48.2 cm,
Albertina, Vienna*

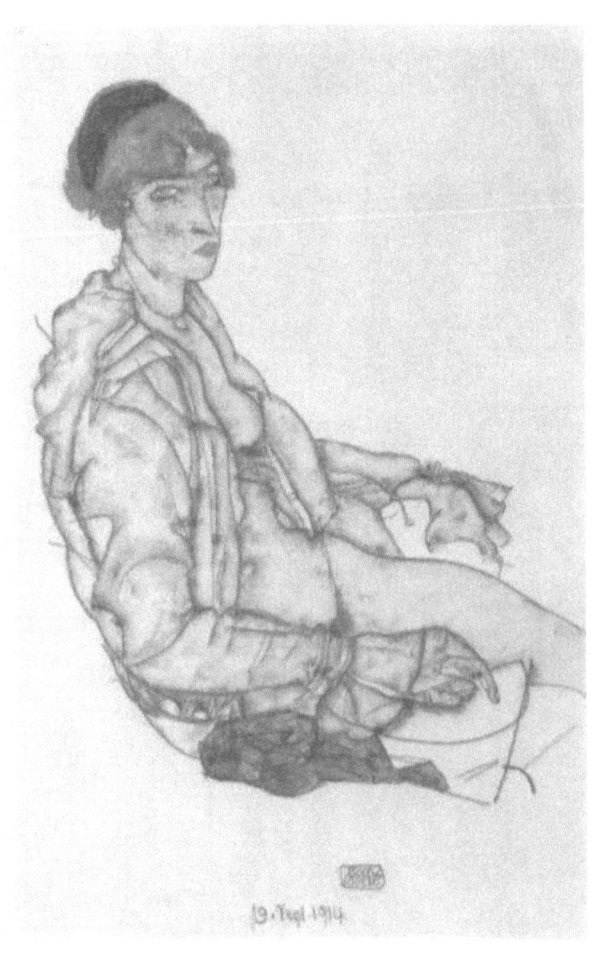

Sitting woman with blue hair ribbon

1914, pencil and watercolor on paper, Leopold Collection

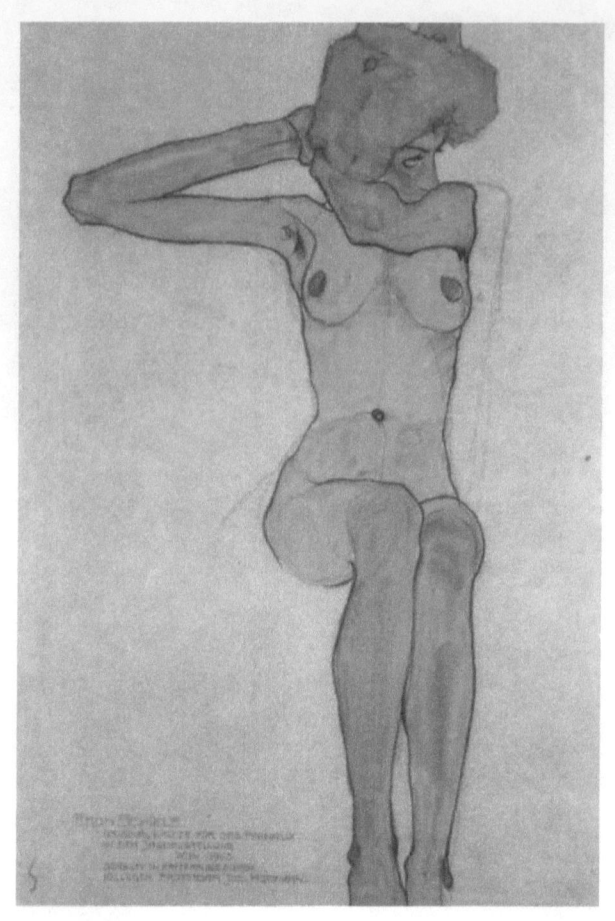

Seated female nude

1910, charcoal, watercolor, Public collection

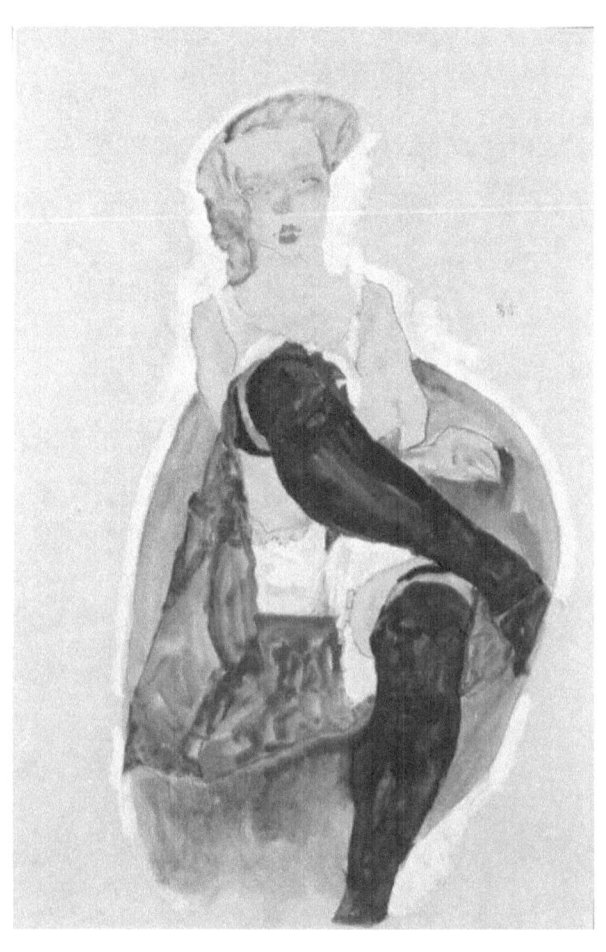

Girl with crossed legs

1911, pencil and gouache on paper, Leopold Museum

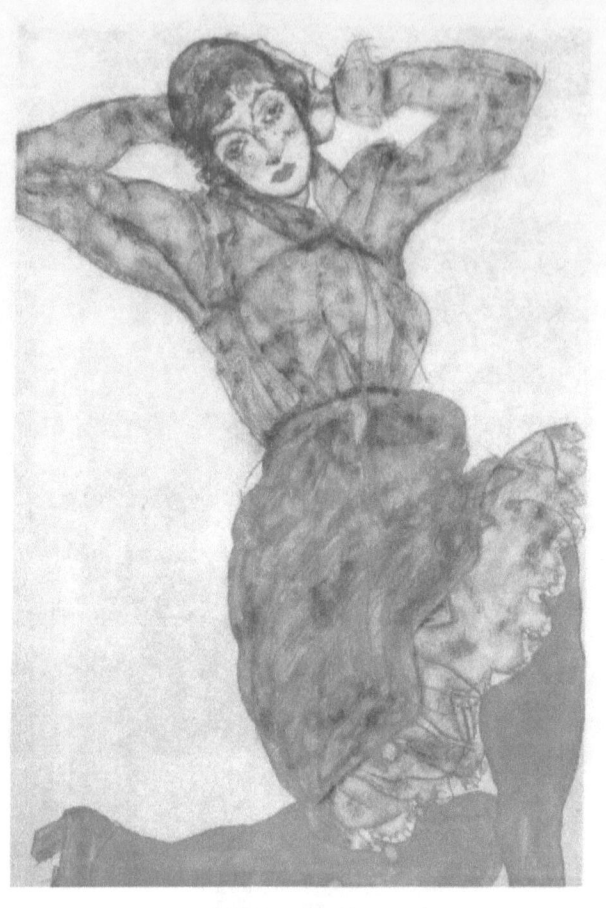

Woman with orange stockings

Unknown date, charcoal, watercolor, Public collection

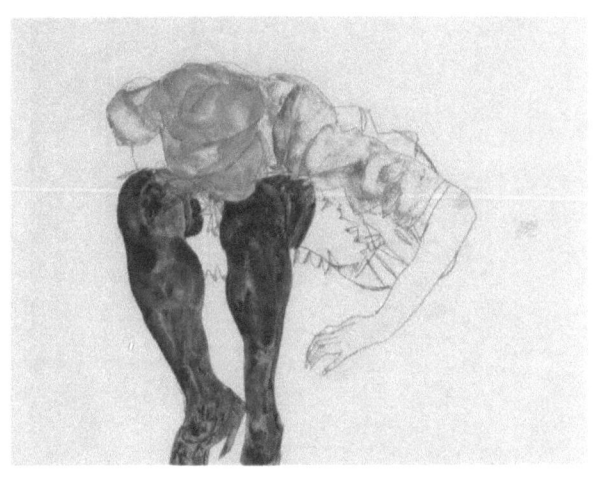

Blonde, leaning forward

1912, pencil, watercolor and gouache on paper, Private collection

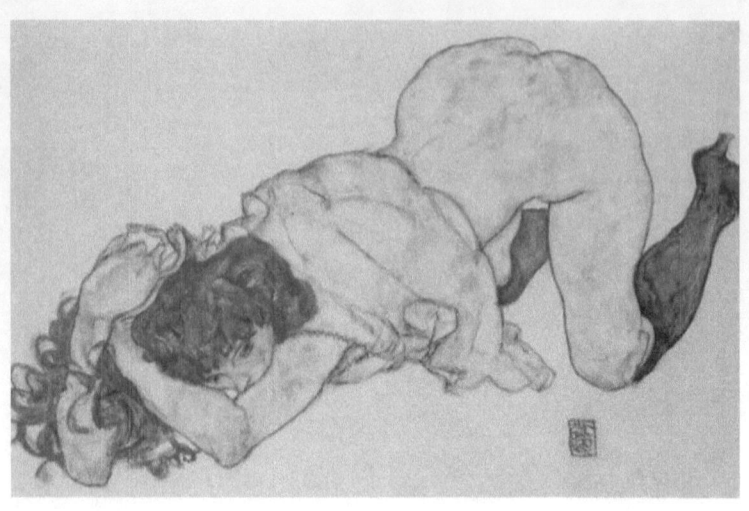

Kneeling girl trimmed on both elbows

1917, chalk on paper, 28.7 x 44.3 cm, Leopold Collection, Vienna

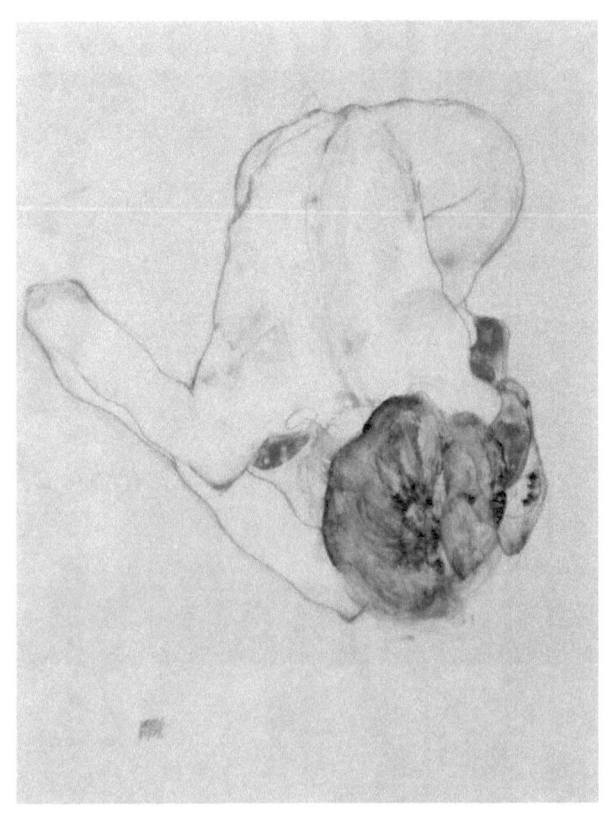

Forward flexed female nude

*1912, pencil and watercolor on paper, 37.5 x 28.9 cm,
Leopold Collection, Vienna*

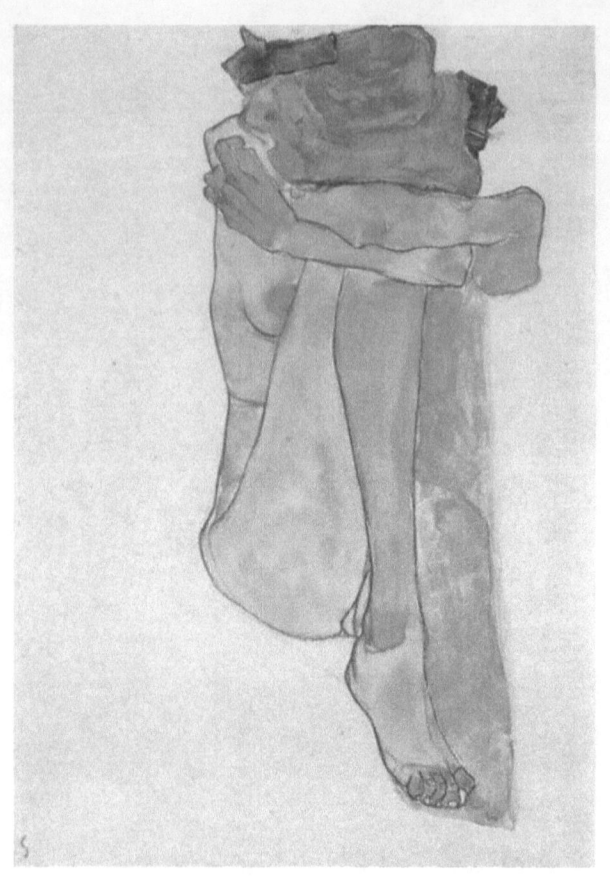

Female Nude with green upholstery

*1910, charcoal, watercolor, 44.9 x 32.2 cm, Neue Galerie
Graz am Landesmuseum Joanneum, Graz*

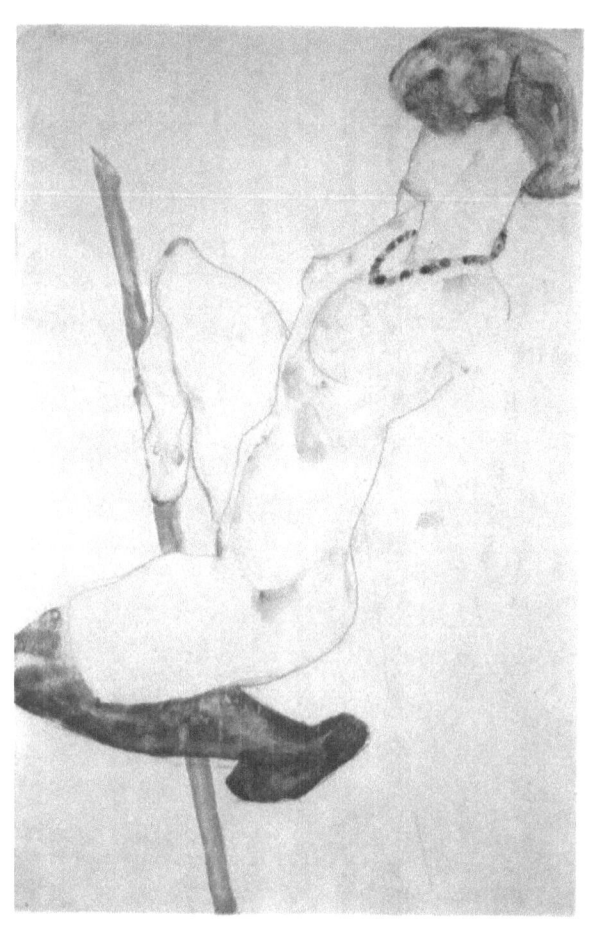

Crouching female nude with bended head

1918, Private collection

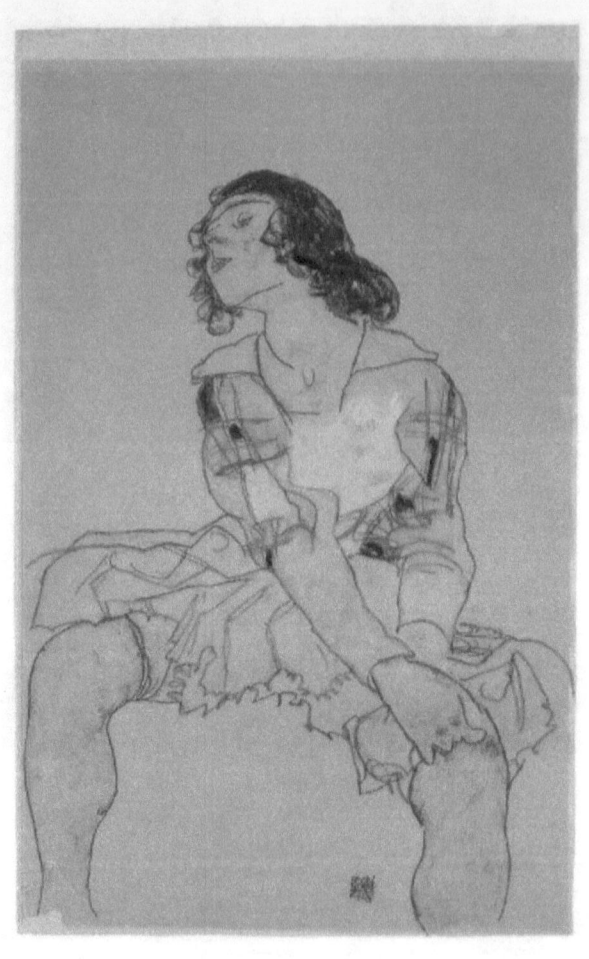

Seating woman

1813, charcoal, watercolor, Private collection

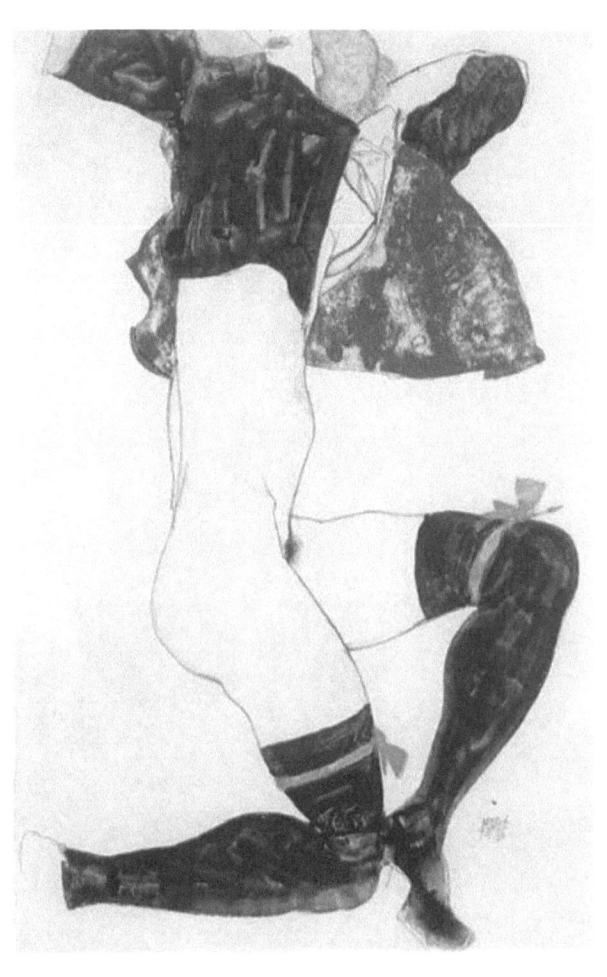

Black Tights

1913, pencil, gouache, 48.3 x 31.4 cm, Private collection

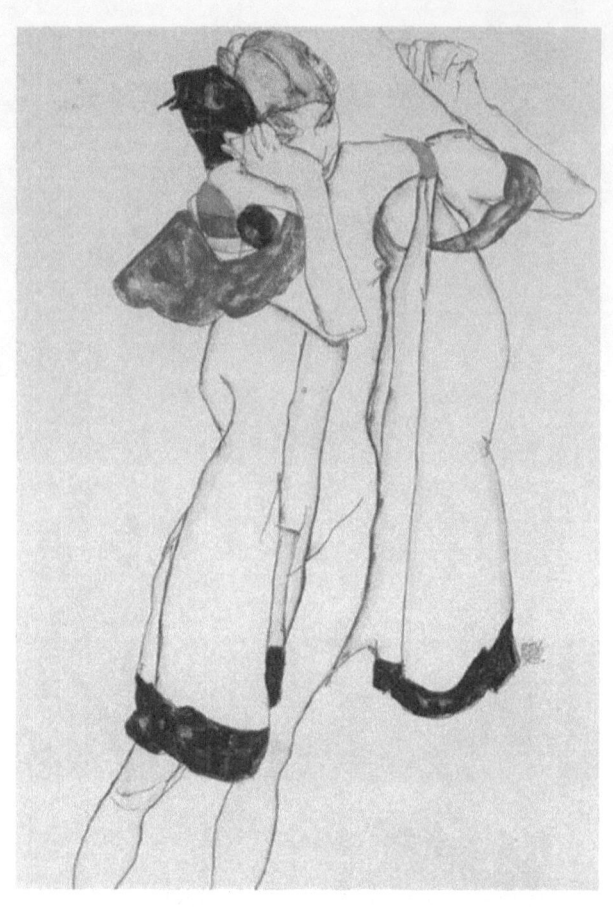

Woman in a Dressing Gown

1913, pencil, watercolor, gouache, 44 x 31 cm, Private collection

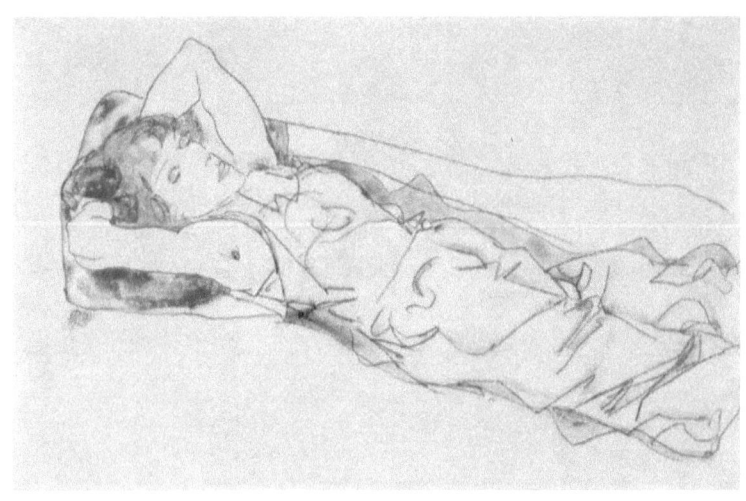

Reclining female figure with gold blonde hair on a blue pillow

1913, pencil, watercolor, gouache, 44 x 31 cm, Private collection

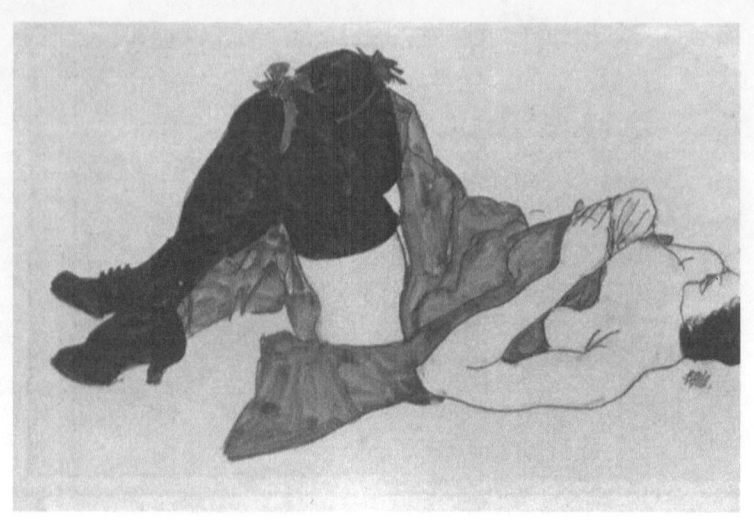

Reclining woman with ochre blanket

1913, pencil, watercolor, gouache, Private collection

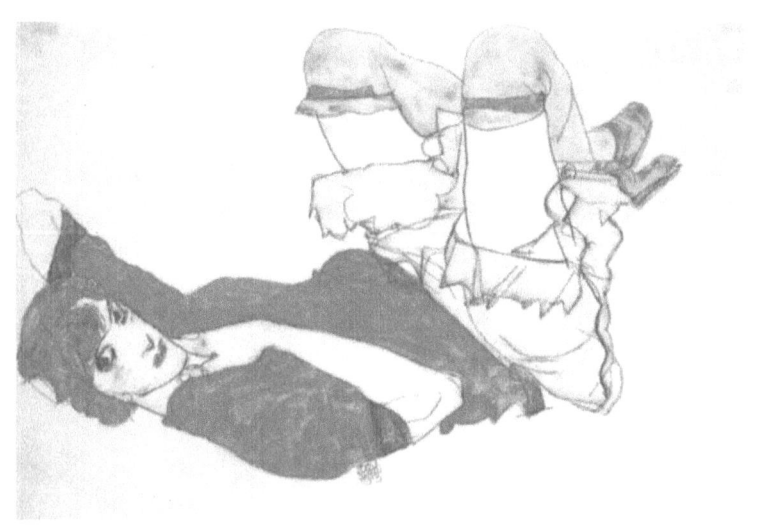

Wally with a Red Blouse

Circa 1913, Watercolor and pencil on paper, Private collection

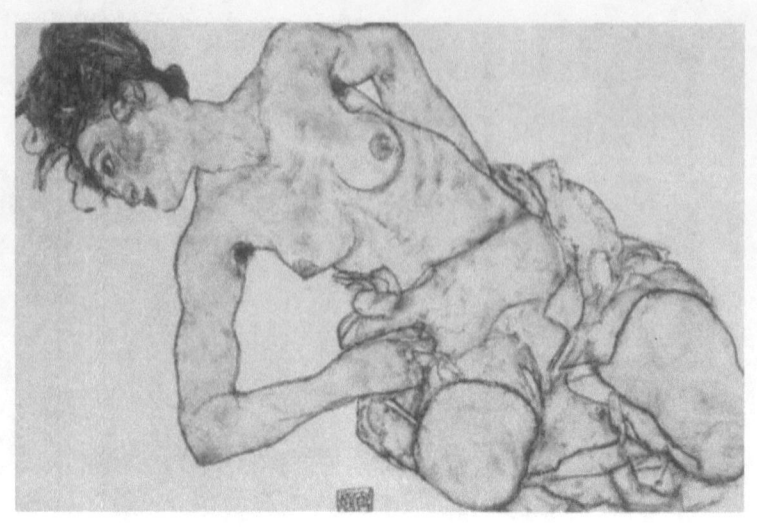

Female semi nude, kneeling

1917, Watercolor and pencil on paper, Private collection

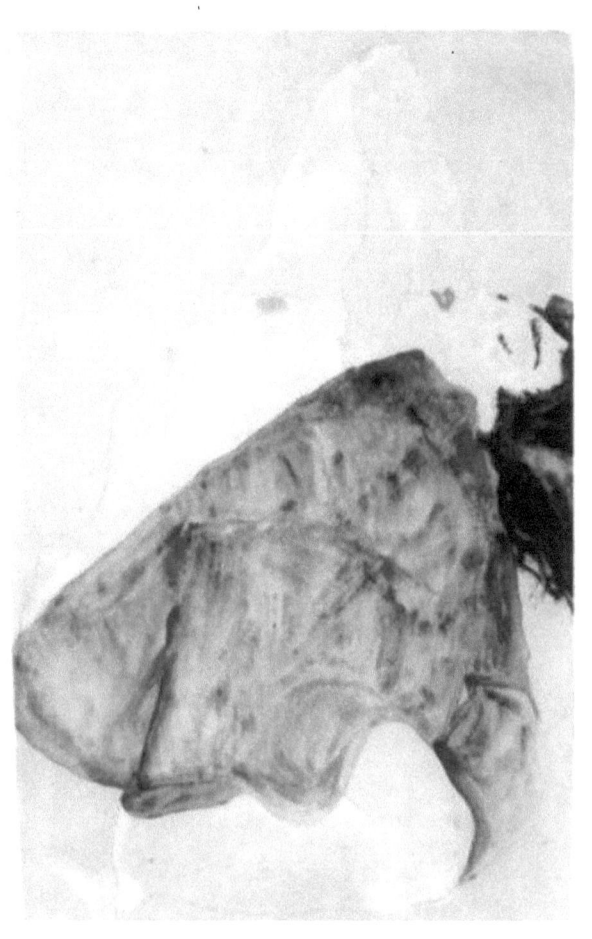

Reclining Nude with purple cloth

1911, Watercolor and pencil on paper, Private collection

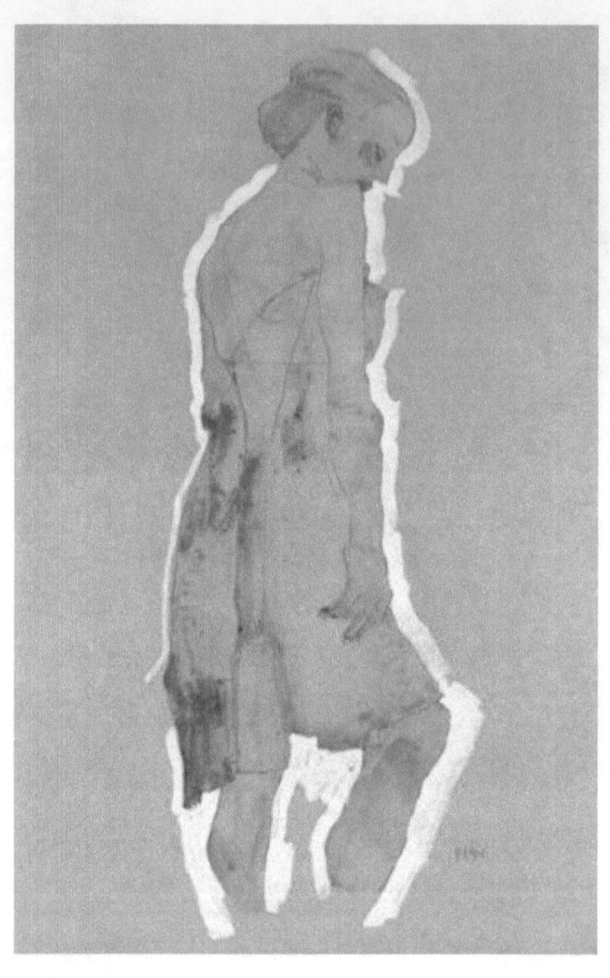

Standing Girl in Profile

1911, Watercolor and pencil on paper, Private collection

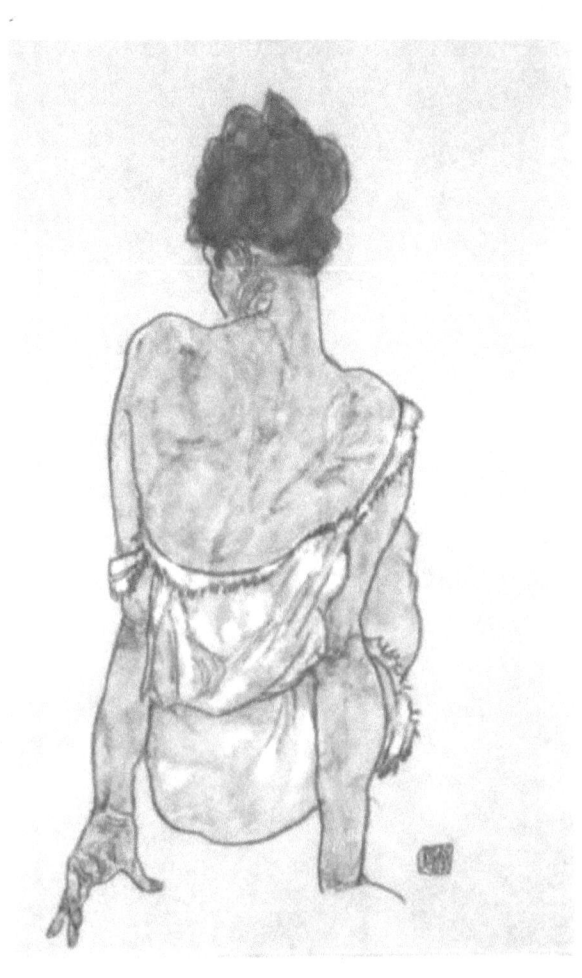

Seating woman

Pencil, watercolor, gouache, 44 x 31 cm, Private collection

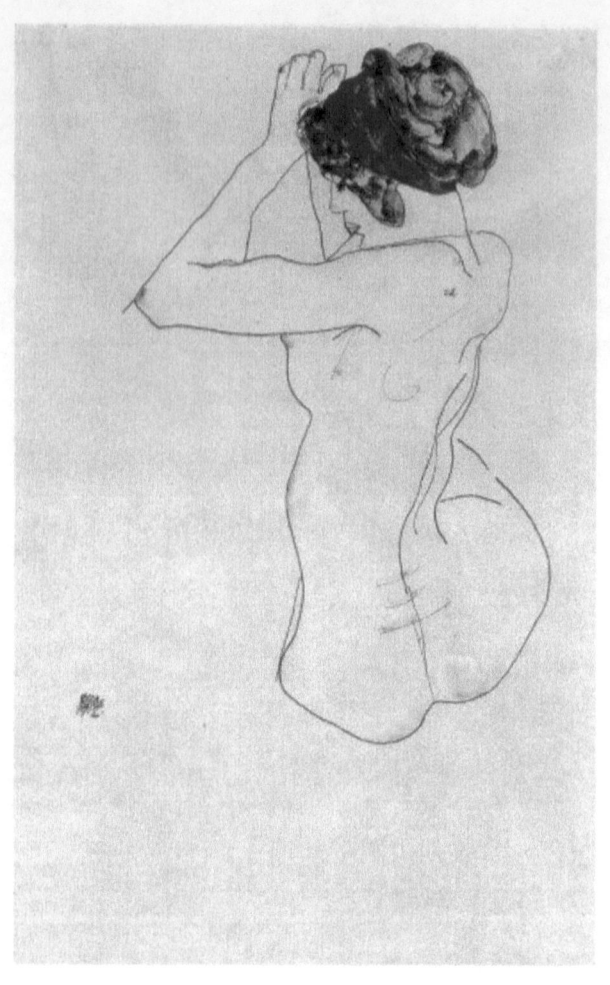

Nude with a Blue Headband

Watercolor and pencil on paper, Private collection

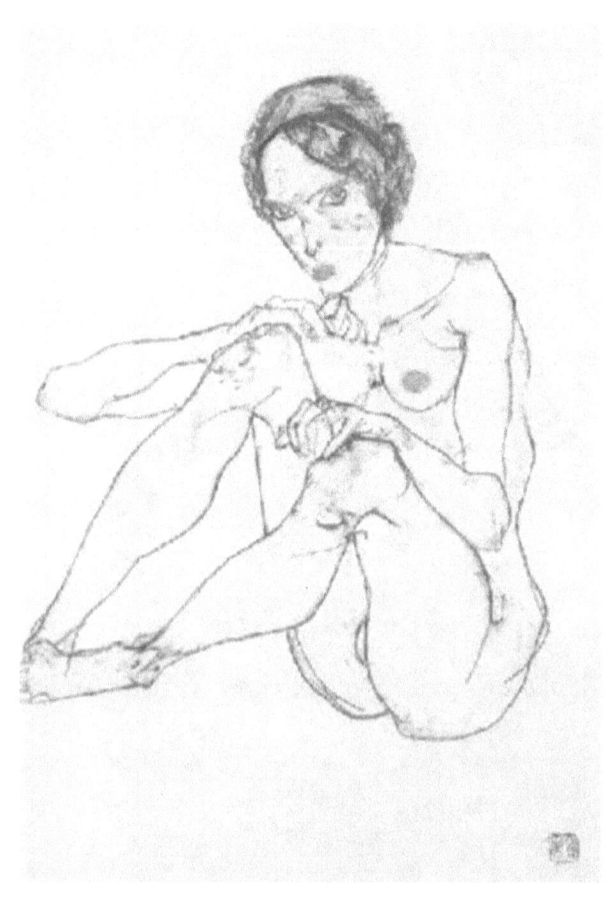

Seated Female Nude

1913, gouache, watercolour and pencil on paper, Private Collection

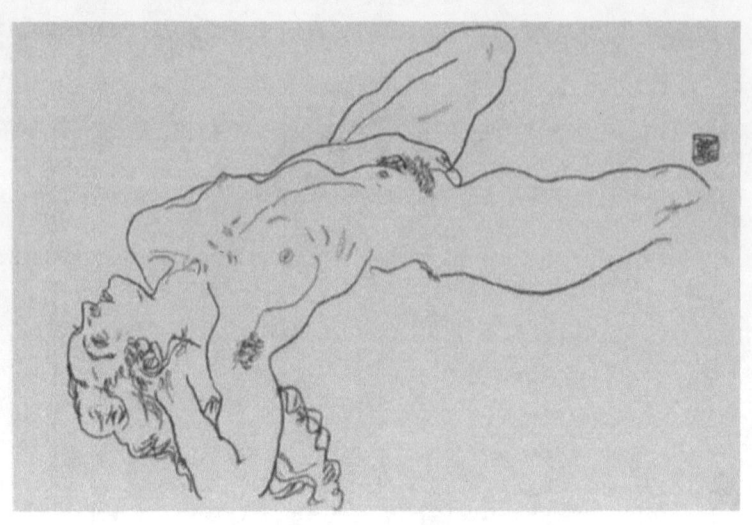

Reclining Nude

1918, black Conte crayon on paper, Private Collection

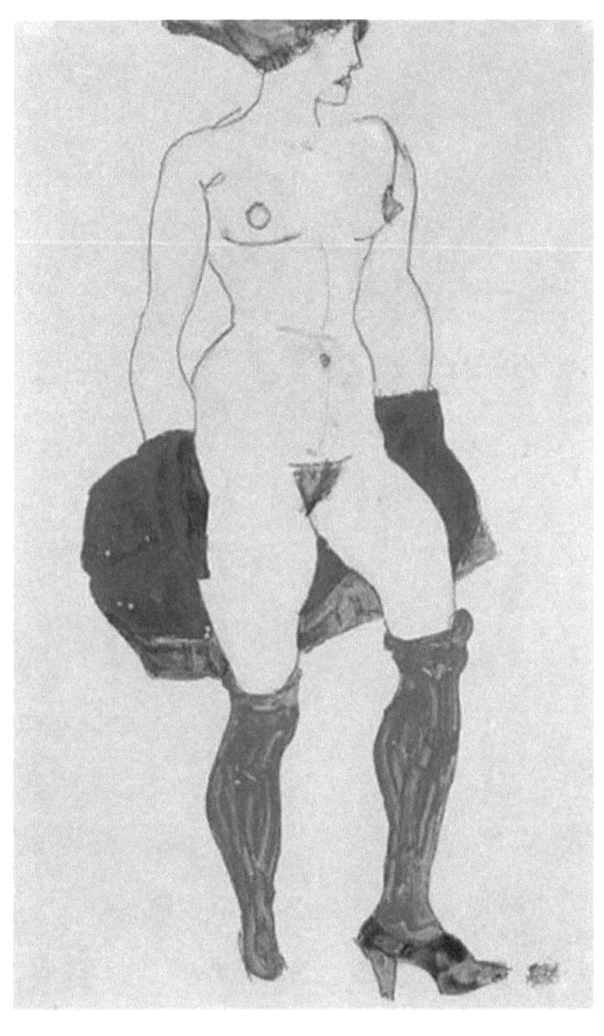

Standing woman with shoes and stockings

1913, gouache, watercolour and pencil on paper, Private Collection

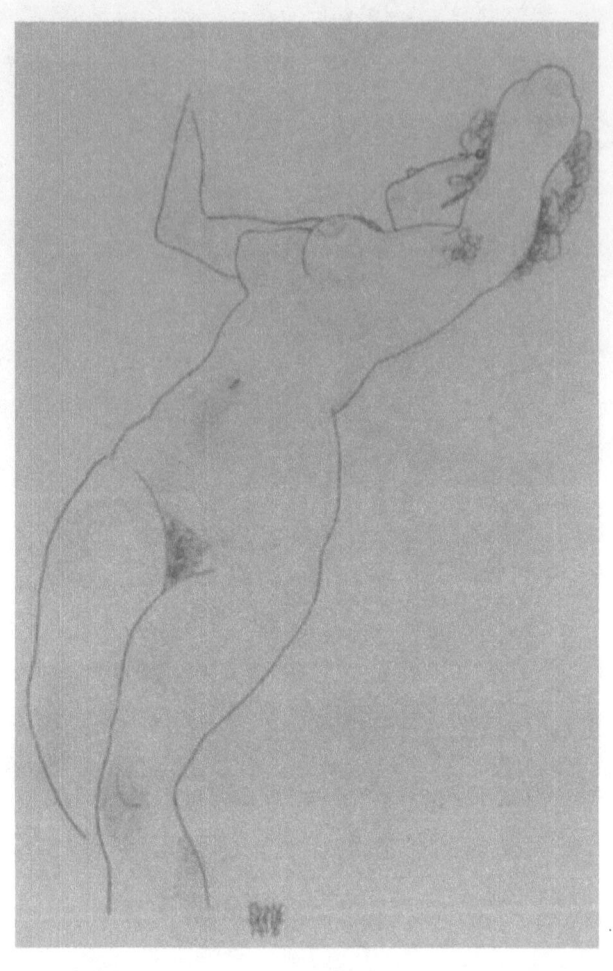

Reclining Nude

1918, pencil and charcoal on paper, Private Collection

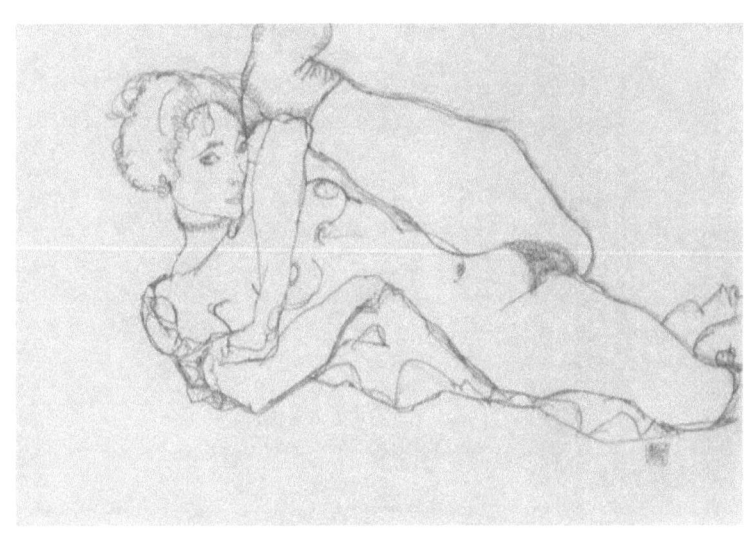

Reclining Nude with left leg tightened

1914, pencil on paper, Private Collection

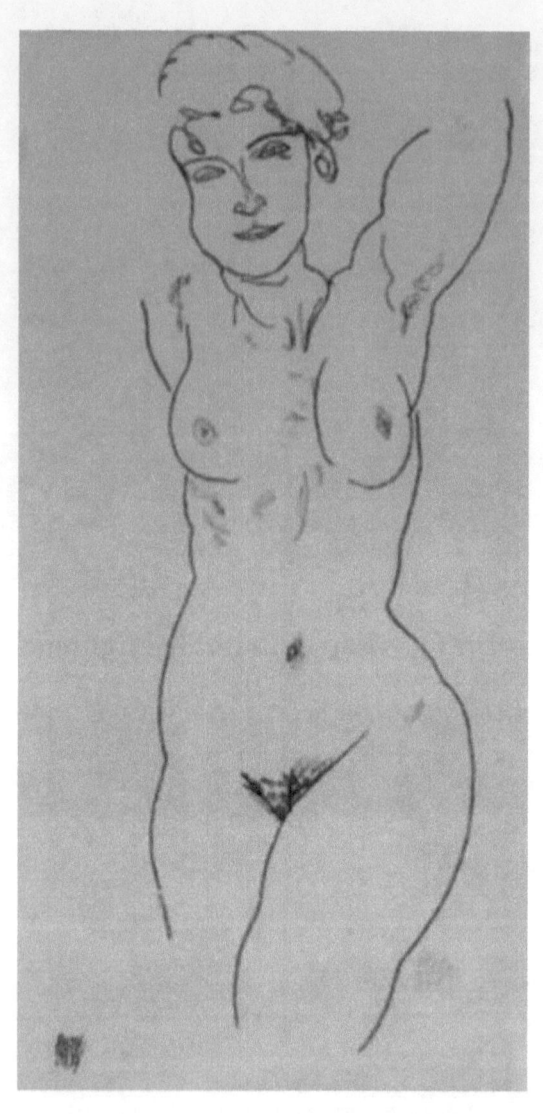

Akt

1917, charcoal on paper, Private Collection

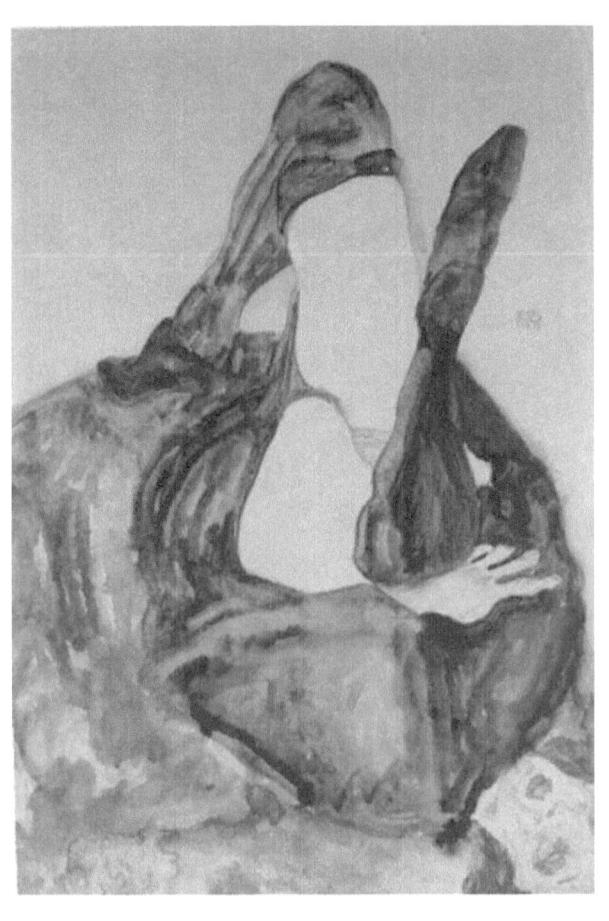

Woman with outstretched leg and purple tights

1911, gouache, watercolour and pencil on paper, Private Collection

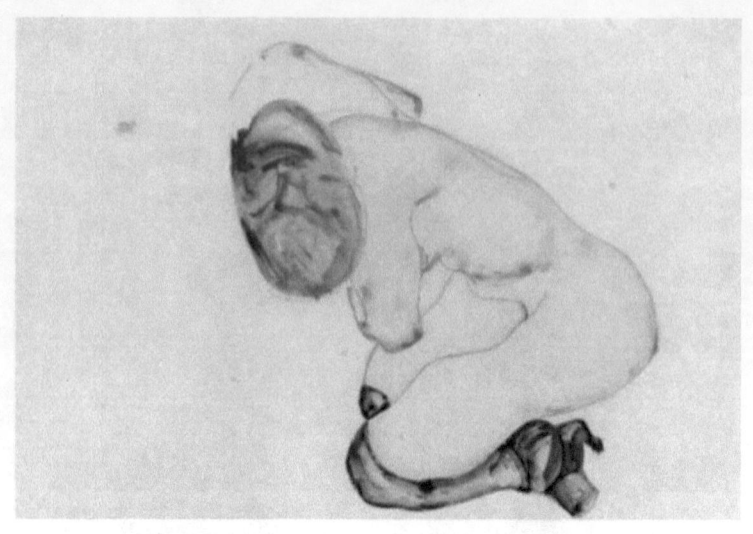

Young girl crouching

1914, watercolor and pencil on paper, Private Collection

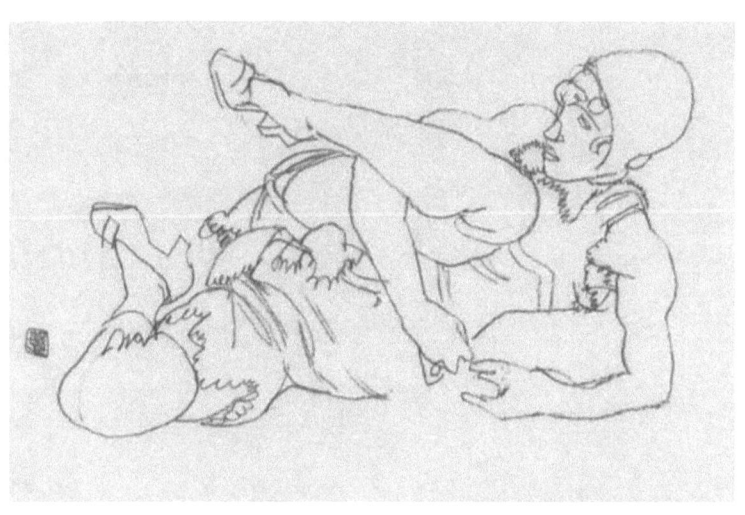

Lying with his right leg tightened

1917, black Conte crayon on paper, Private Collection

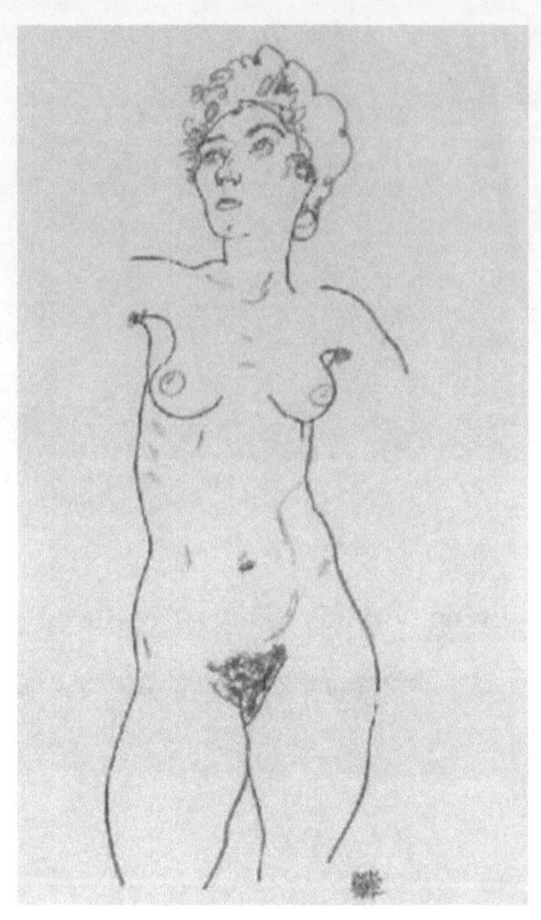

Standing Female Nude, look up

1917, charcoal on paper, Private Collection

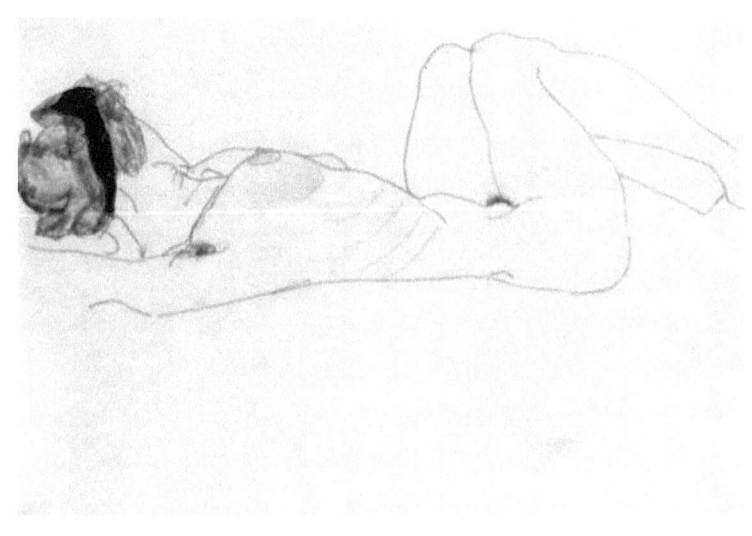

Reclining nude

1912, pencil and watercolour on paper, Private Collection

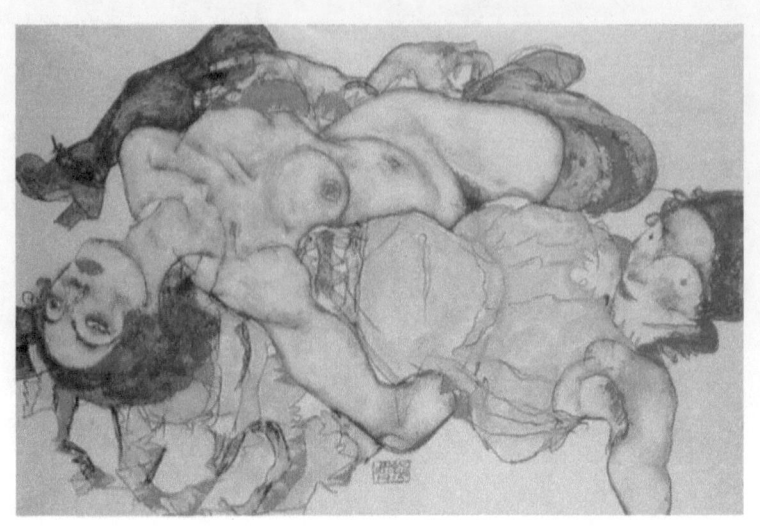

Two Girls Lying Entwined

1915, Gouache and pencil on paper, The Albertina

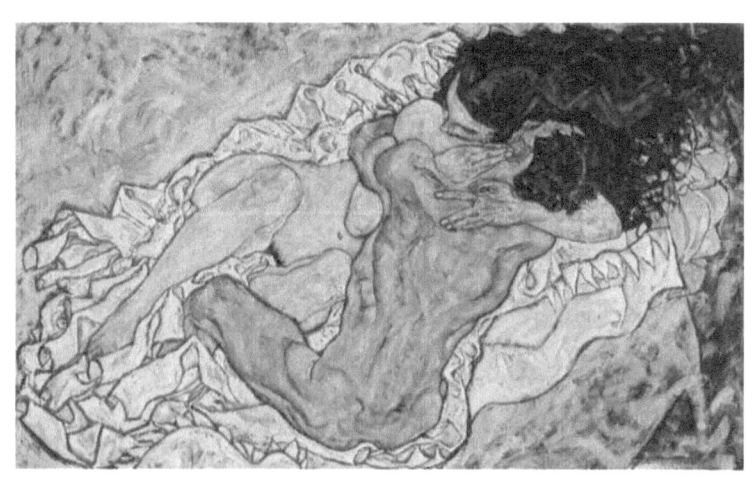

Embrace (also known as Lovers II)

1917, oil on canvas, Osterreichische Galerie Belvedere

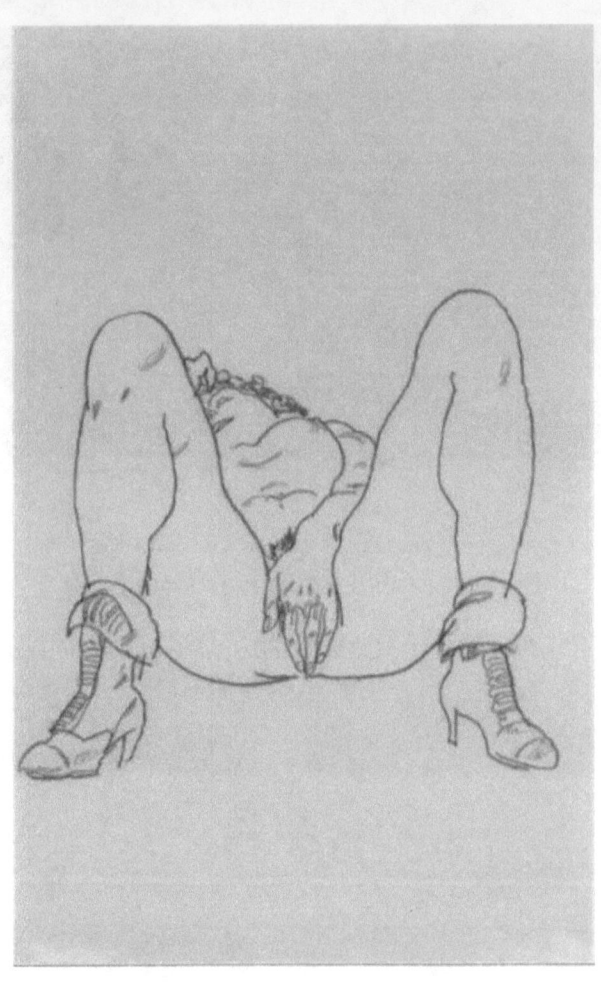

Reclining Nude with Boots

1918, Charcoal on paper, The Metropolitan Museum of Art

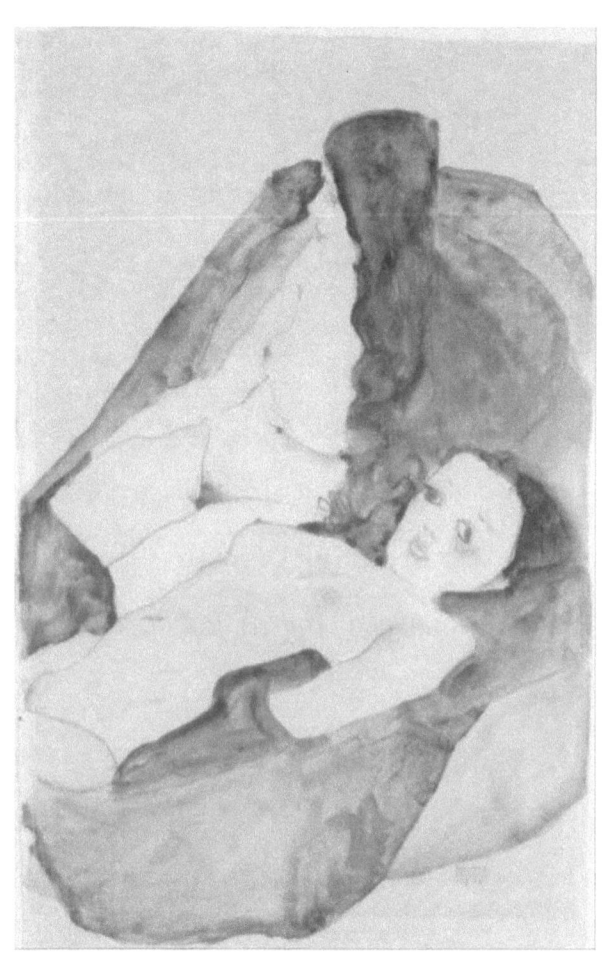

Two Reclining Nudes

1911, Watercolor and graphite on paper, Public collection

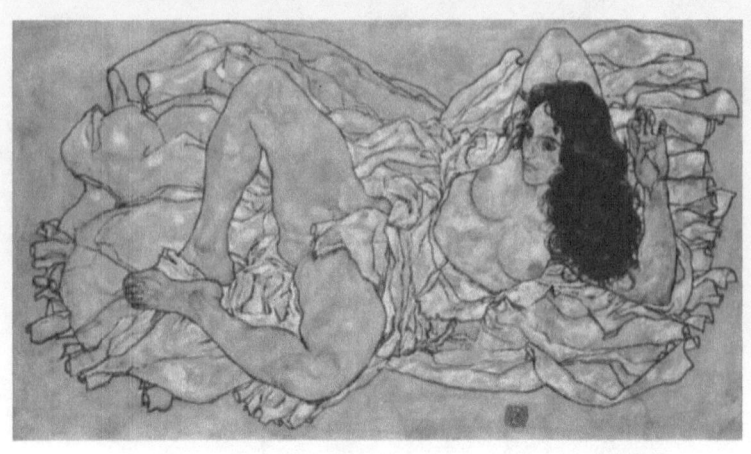

Reclining Woman

1917, Medium oil on canvas, Public collection

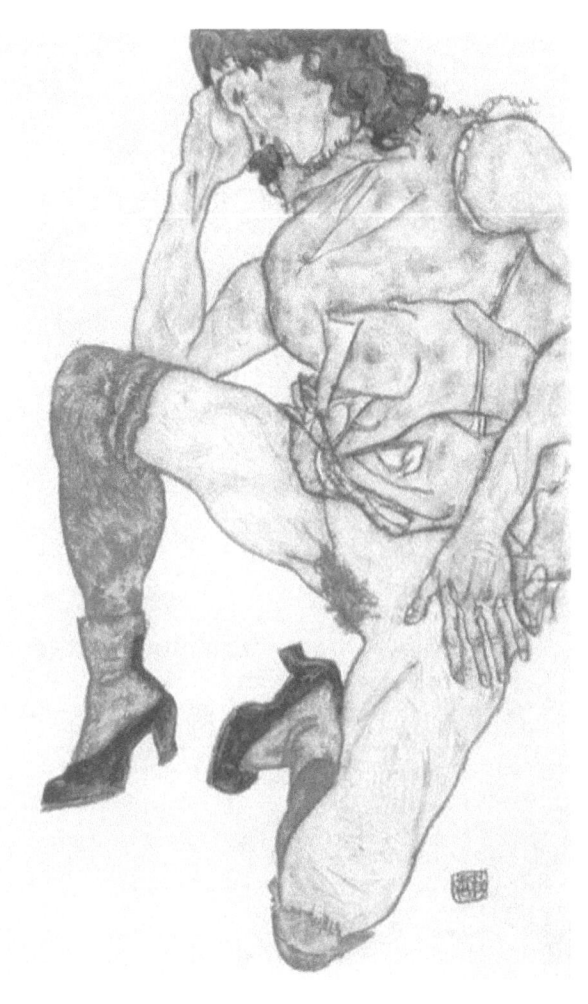

Kneeling girl

1917, Black chalk, gouache, 46 x 28.8 cm, Statliche Graphic Collection, Munchen

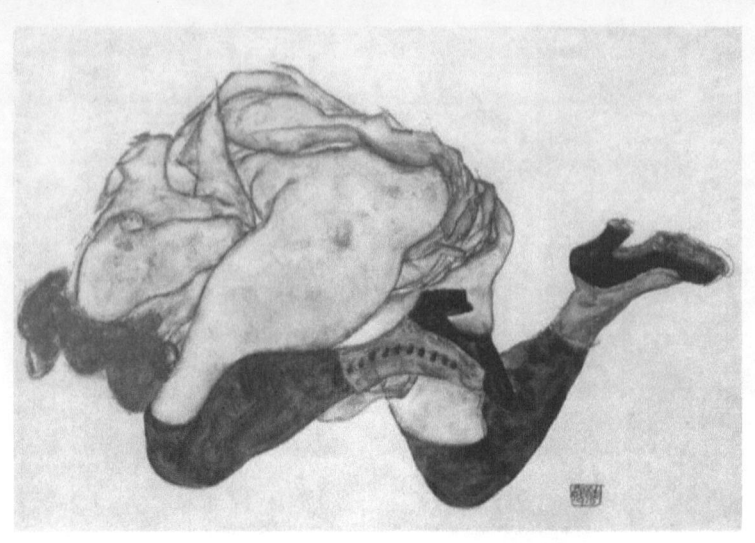

Reclining woman with ochre blanket

1913, pencil, watercolor, gouache, Private collection

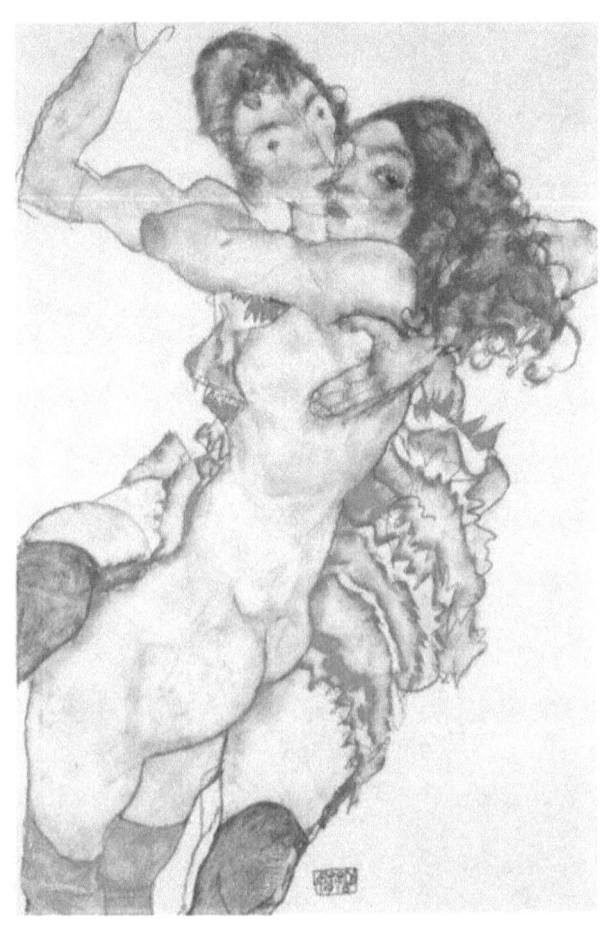

Two Girlfriends

*1915, pencil, watercolor, gouache, 48 x 32.7 cm, Museum of
Fine Arts, Budapest*

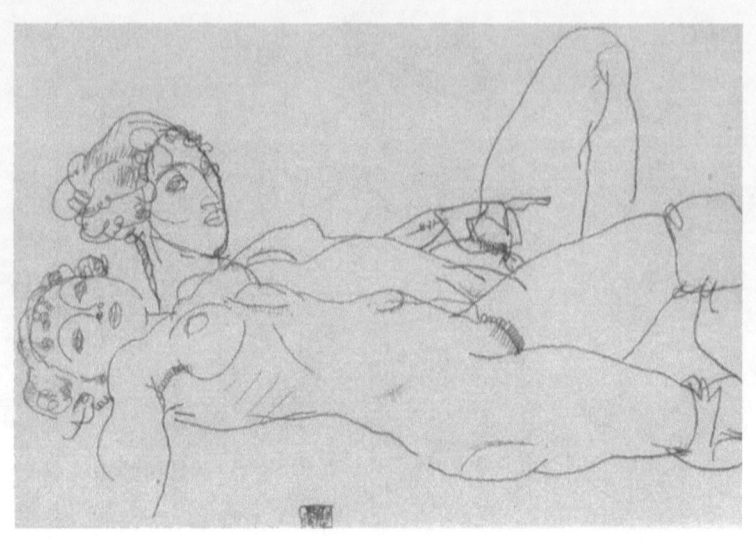

Two lying girls' nudes

*1914, pencil on brown paper, 31 x 46.5 cm, Peter Infeld
Private Foundation, Vienna*

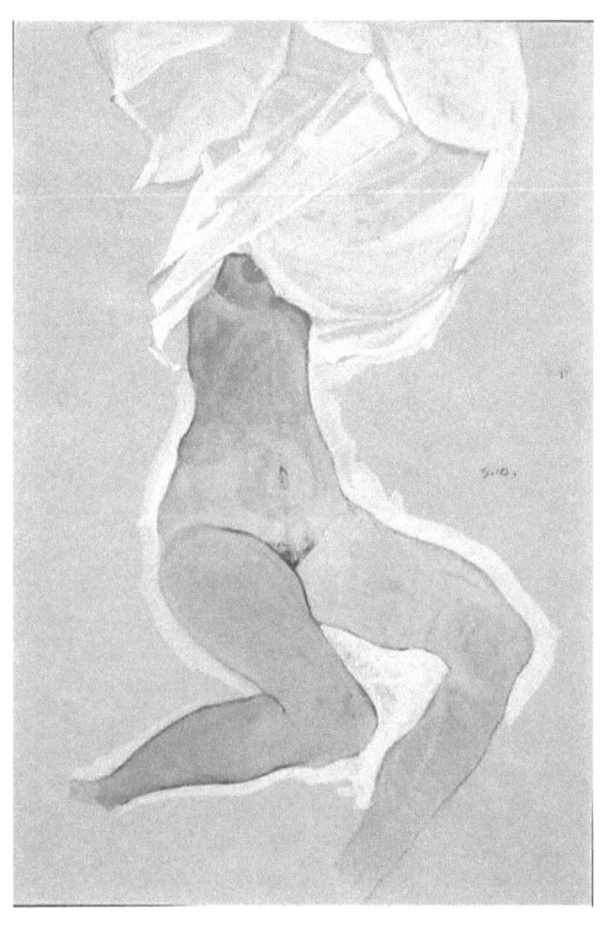

Sitting nude girl with a shirt over her head

*1910, pencil, watercolor on wrapping paper, 44.7 x 32.7 cm,
Albertina, Vienna*

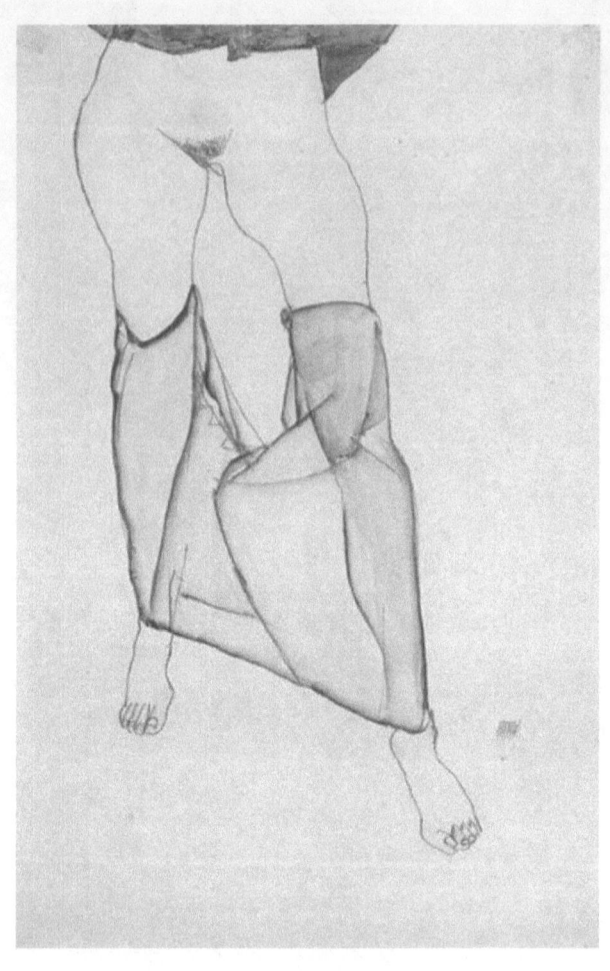

Female Torso with green drapery

1913, watercolor, gouache, pencil on Japan paper, 47.9 x 32 cm, Albertina, Vienna

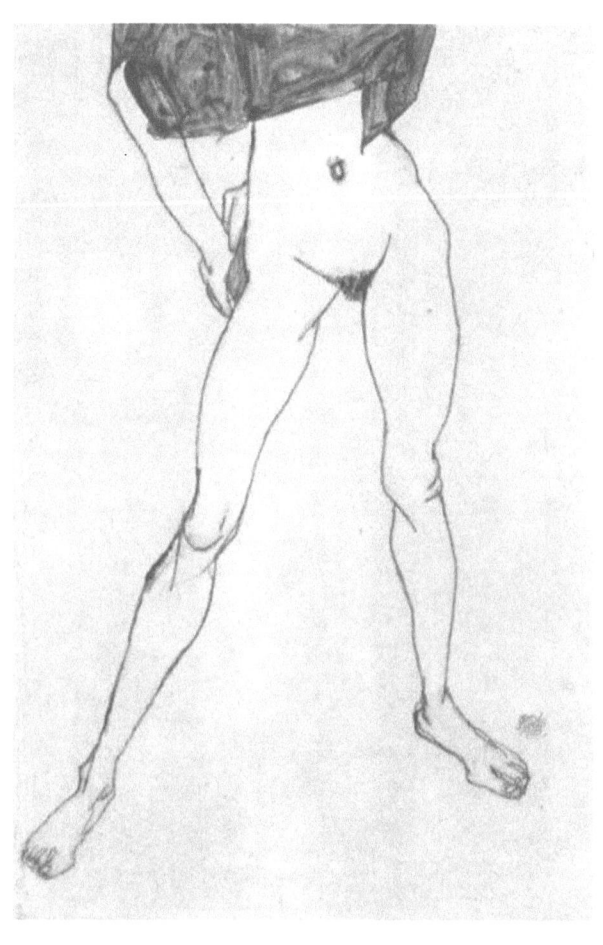

Staying female torso with olive coloured shirt

1913, watercolor and gouache on paper, Private collection

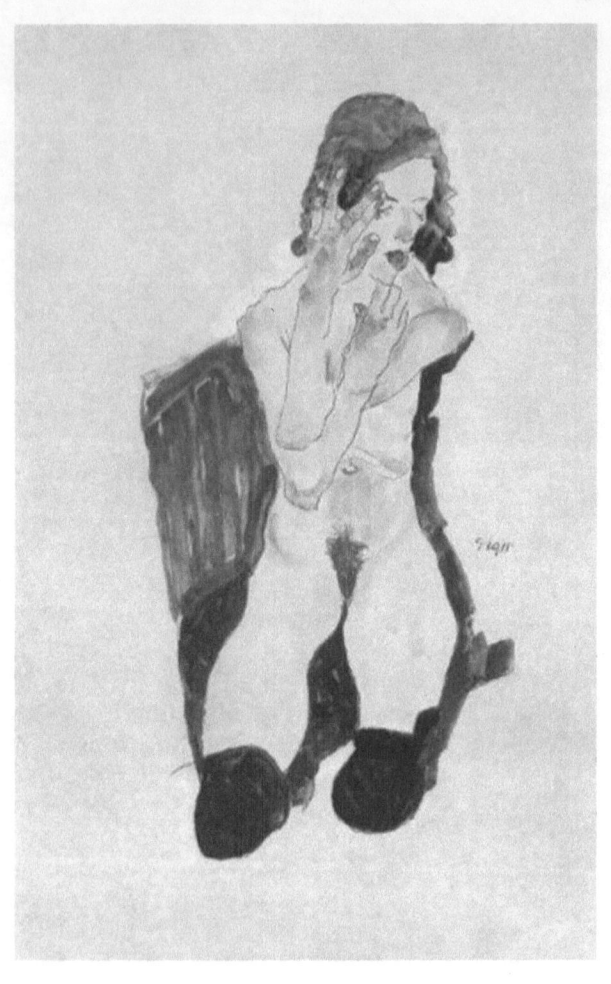

Sitting girl with black tights

1911, gouache, watercolour and pencil heightened with white on paper, Private collection

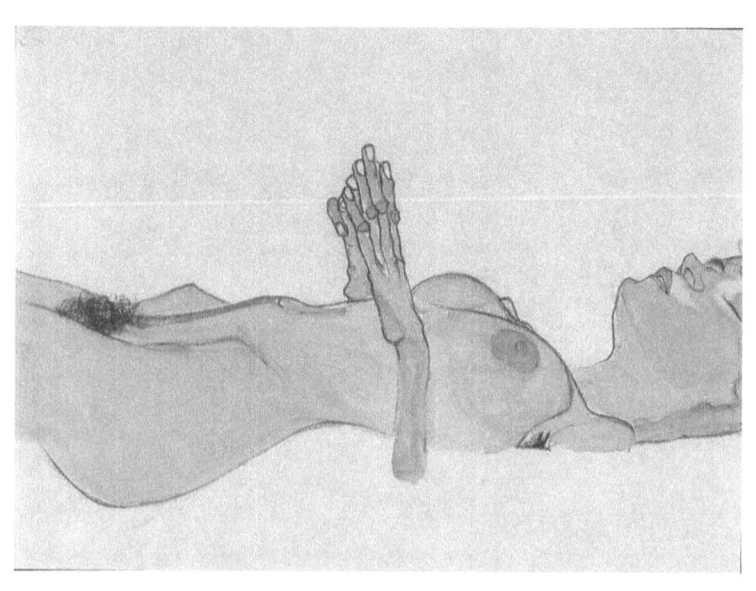

Dead Girl

1910, Watercolor, 30.5 x 44 cm

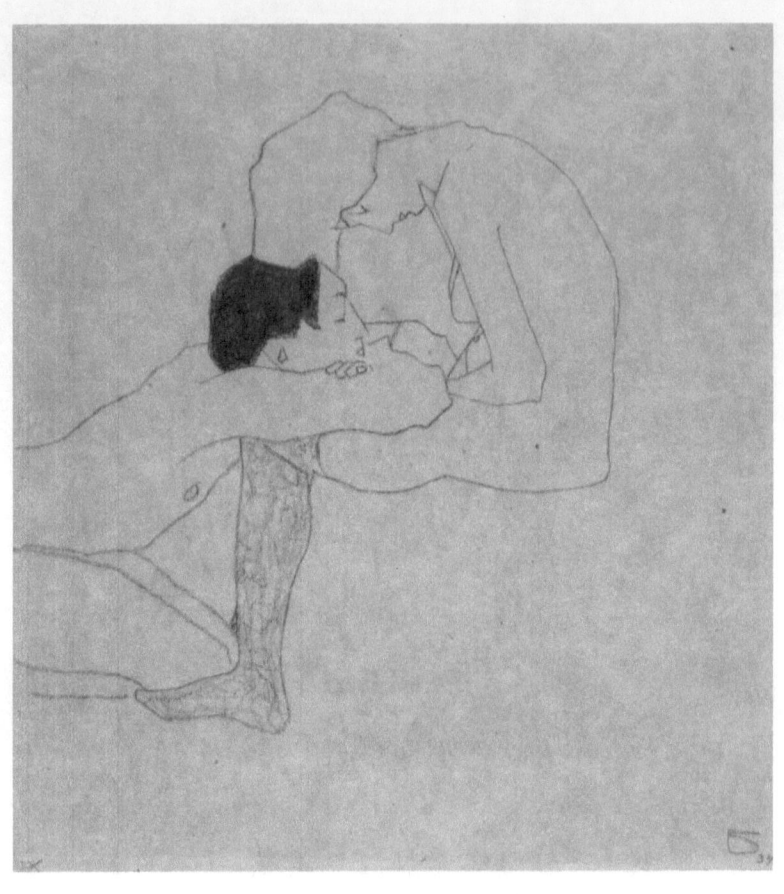

Lovers

1909, Pencil on paper, Private collection

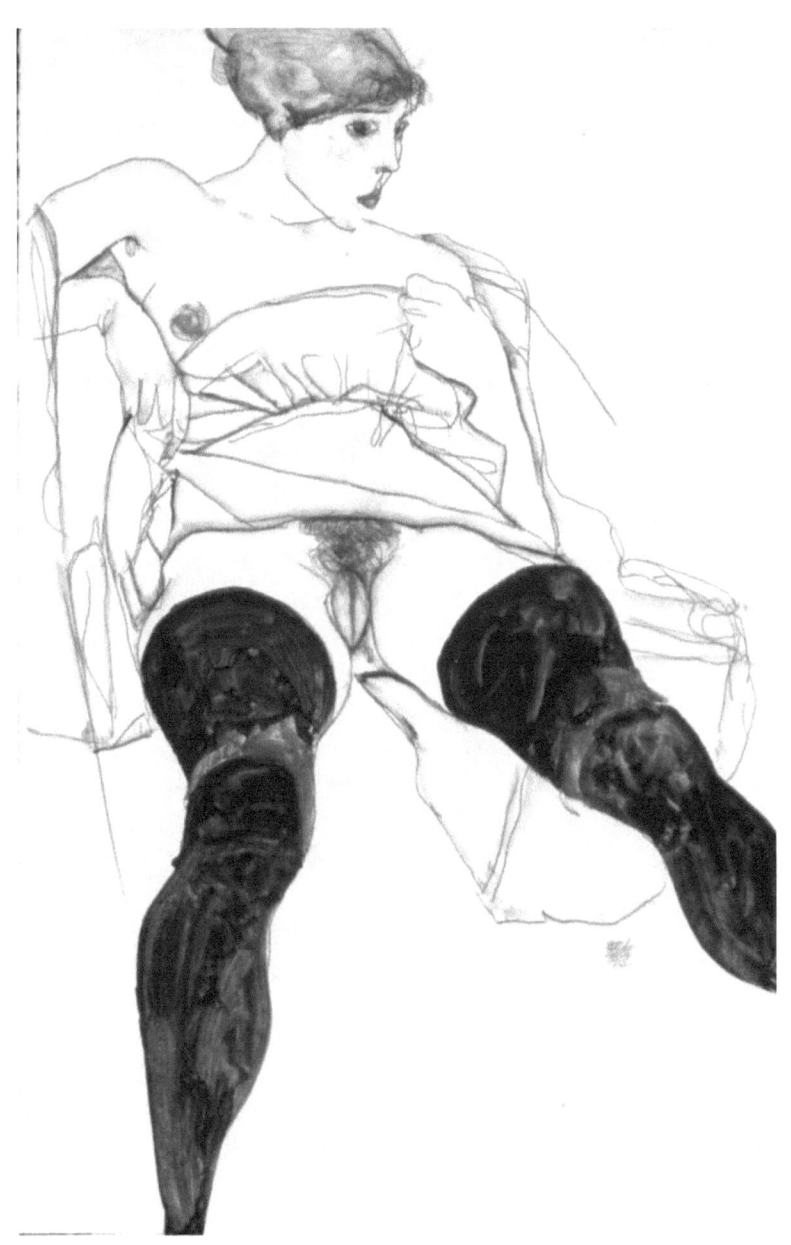

Woman with Black Stockings

1913, Gouache

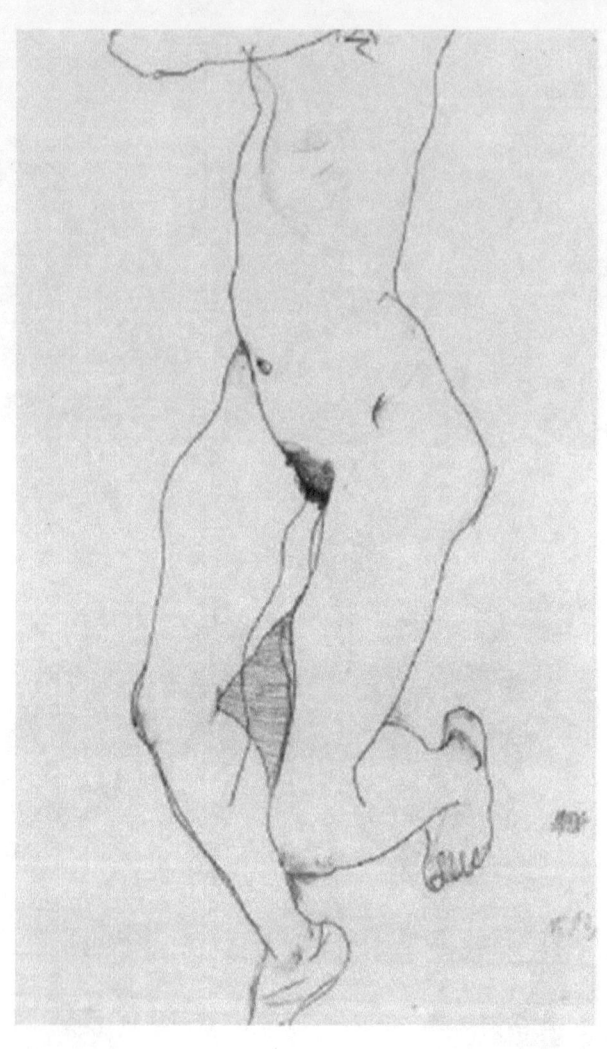

Running Woman

1913, watercolour and pencil on paper, Private collection

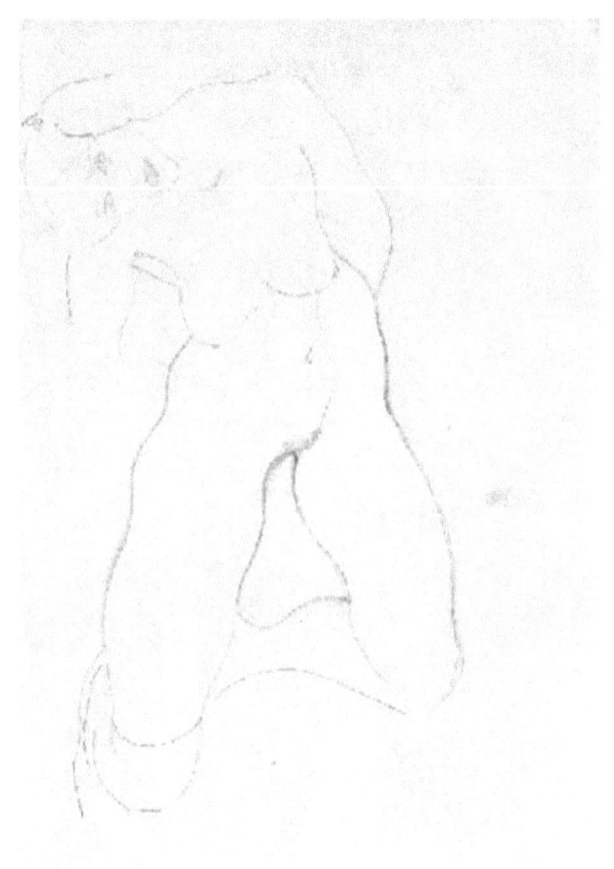

Kneeling female nude

1912, pencil on paper, Private collection

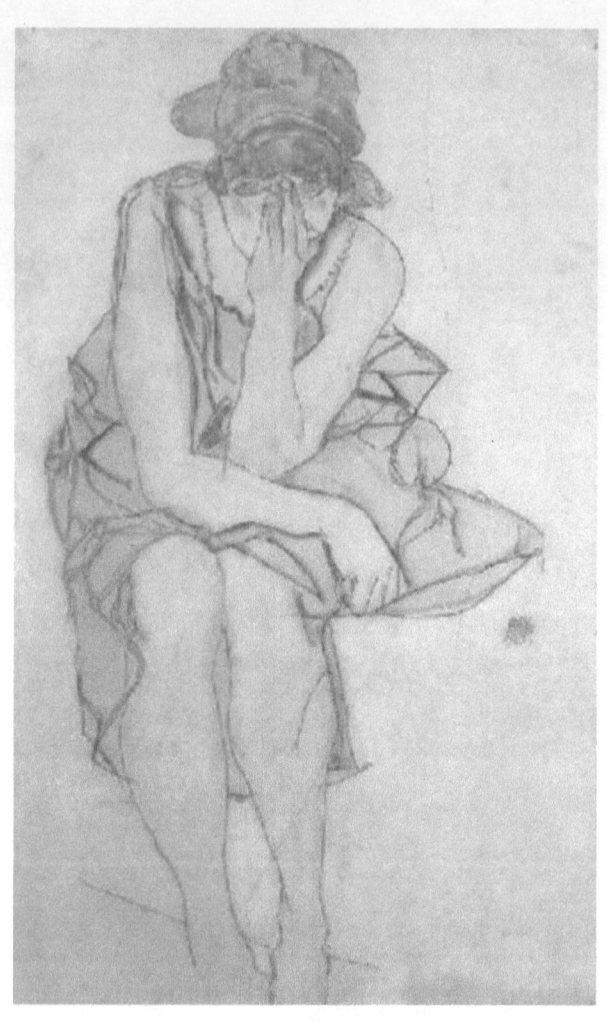

Sitting woman with blond hair

1913, pencil on paper; gouache and watercolour probably added by another hand, Private collection

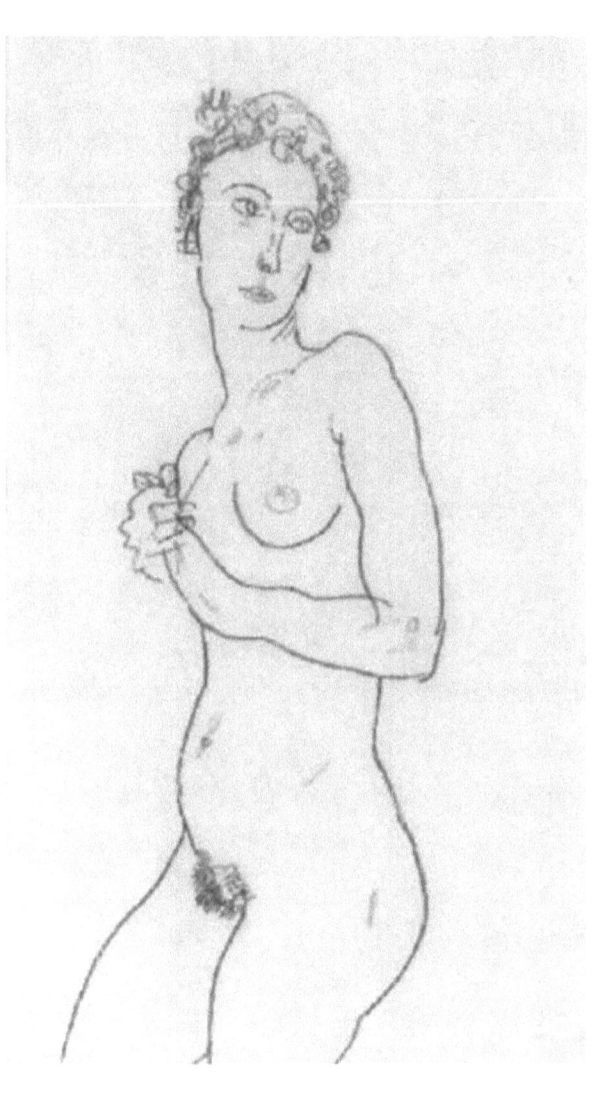

Standing Nude

1918, black Conte crayon on paper, Private collection

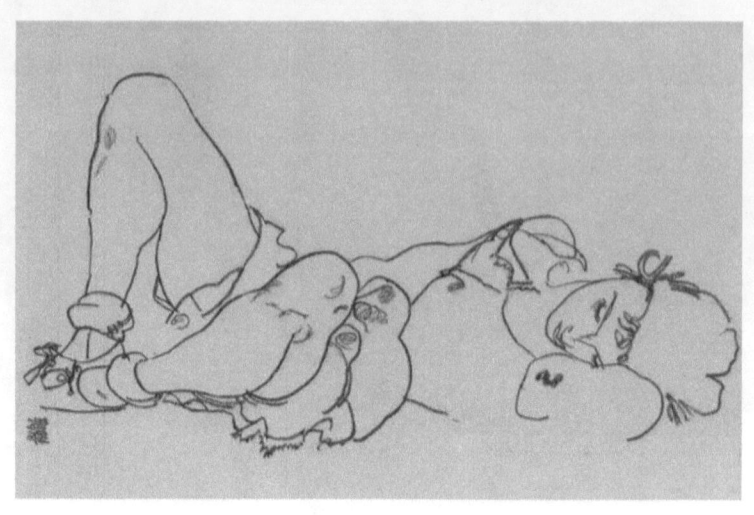

Lying

1918, black crayon on paper, Private collection

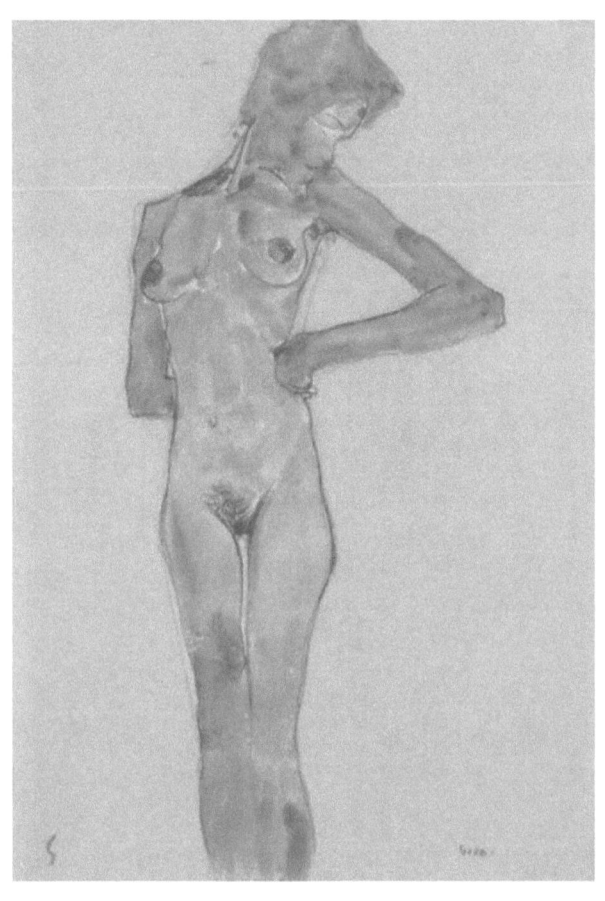

Standing Female Nude (Gerti Schiele)

n.d., watercolor and charcoal on paper, Private collection

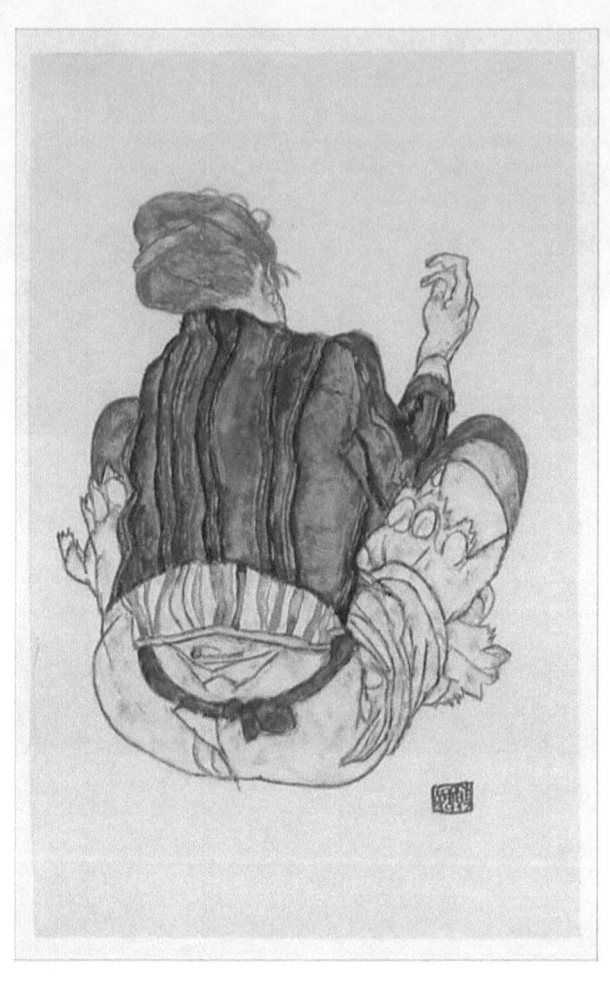

Seated Woman, Back View

1917, Watercolor, gouache, and graphite on paper

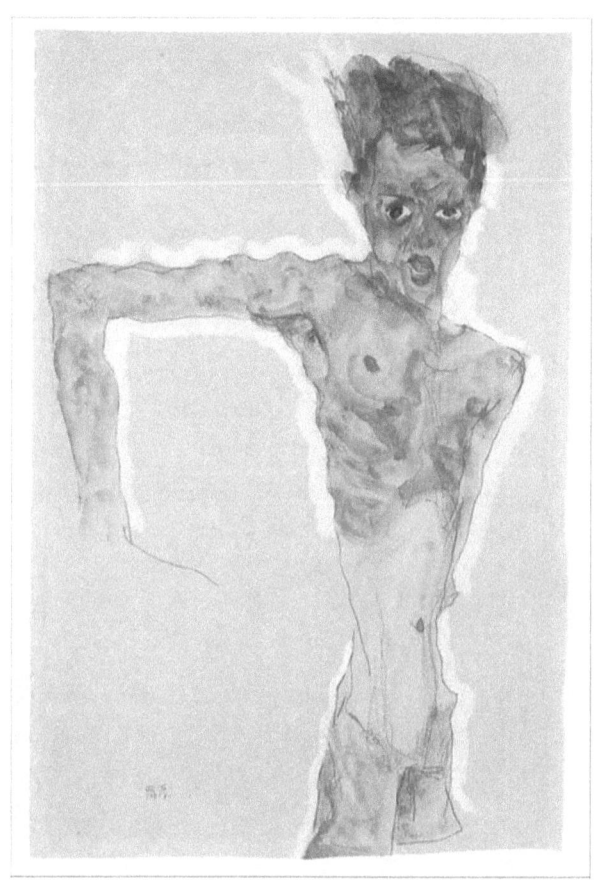

Self-Portrait

1911, Watercolor, gouache, and graphite on paper

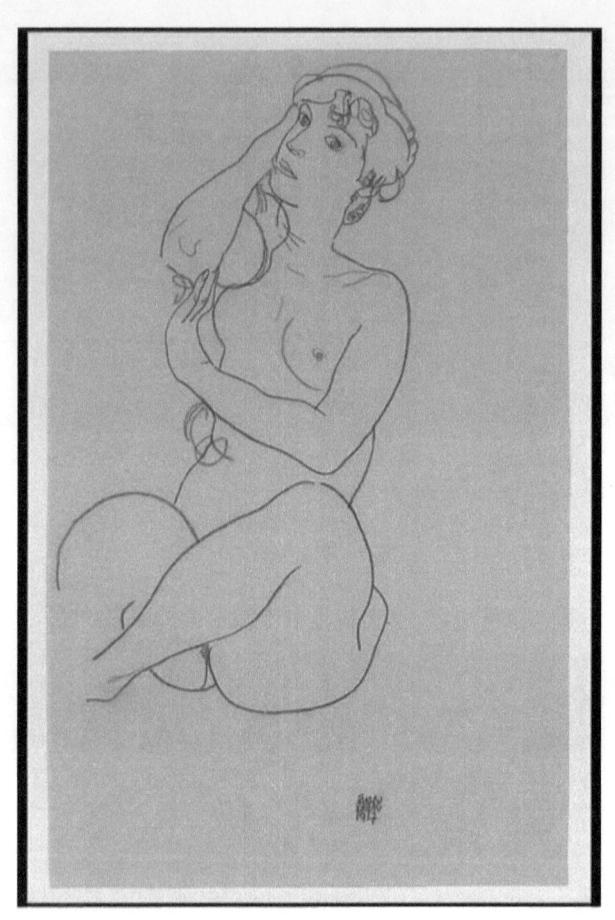

Reclining Nude

1917, Charcoal on paper

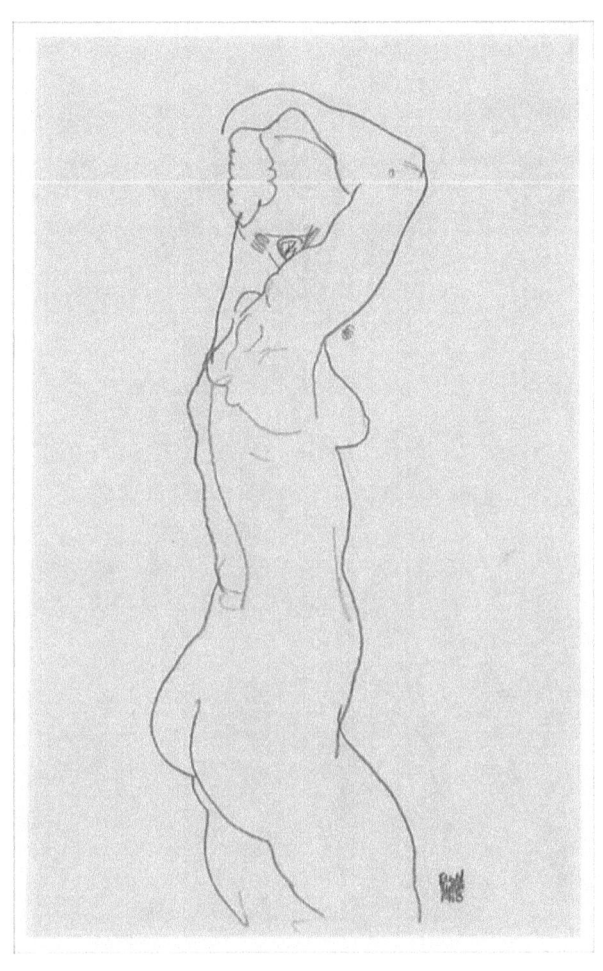

Standing Nude, Facing Right

1918, Charcoal on paper

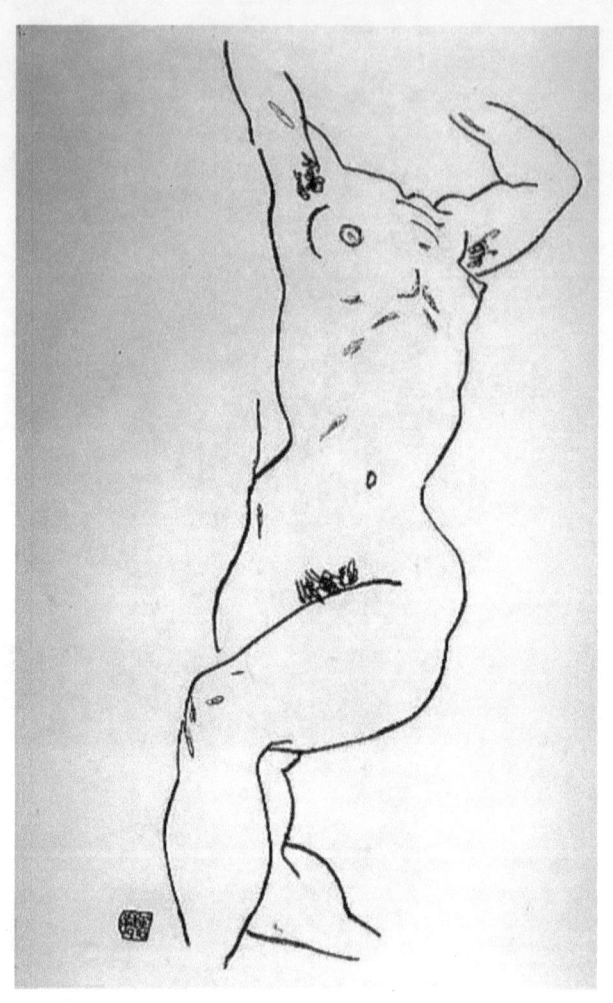

Torso of a Reclining Nude

1918, Charcoal on paper

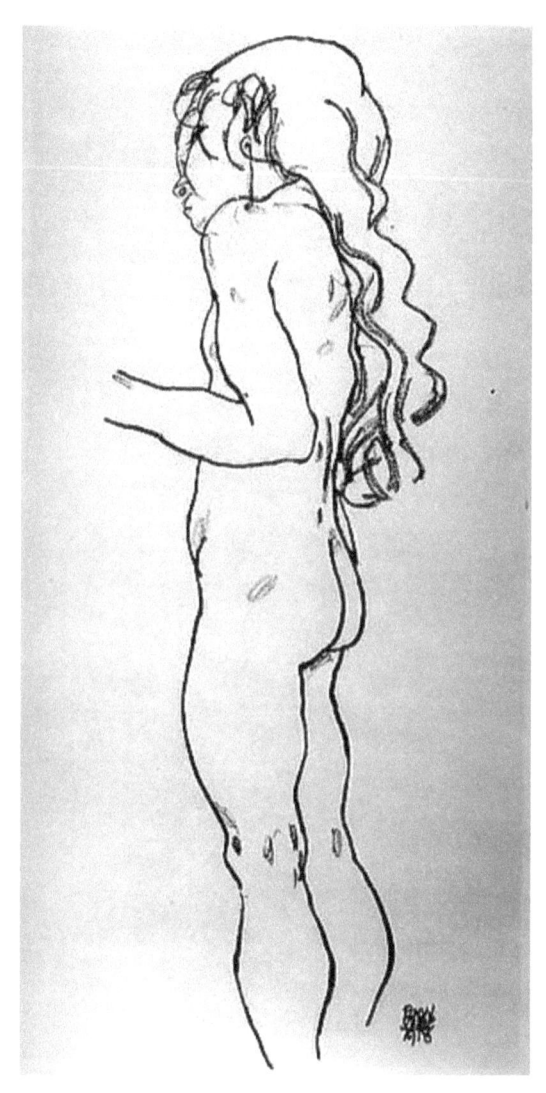

Standing Nude Girl, Facing Left

1918, Charcoal on paper

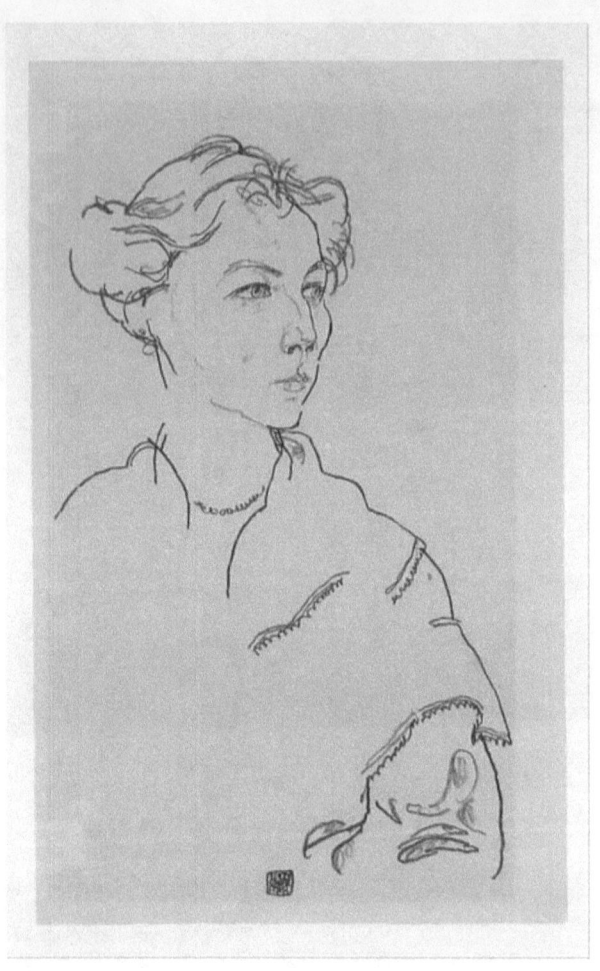

Lilly Steiner

1918, Charcoal on paper

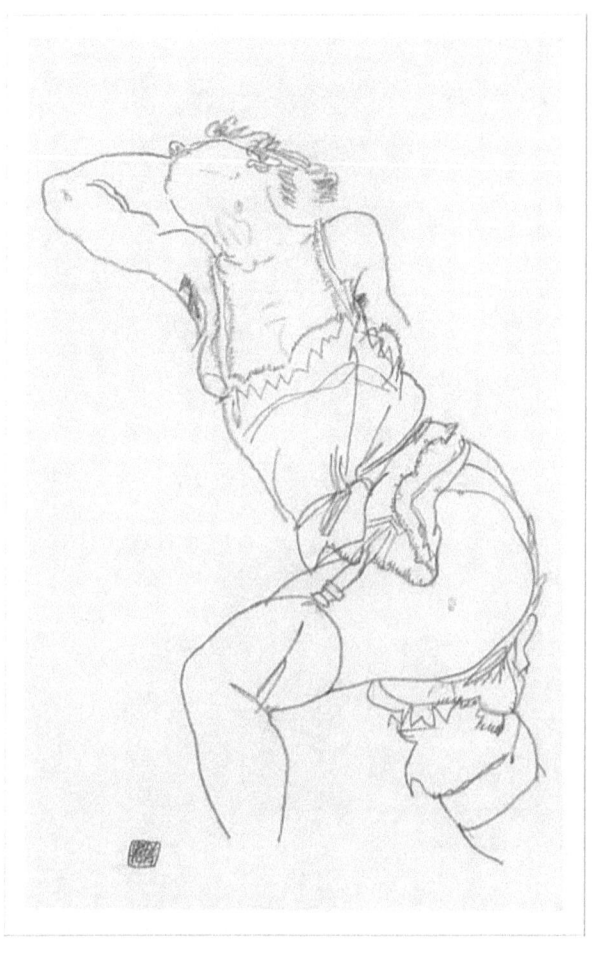

Reclining Model in Chemise and Stockings

1917, Charcoal on paper

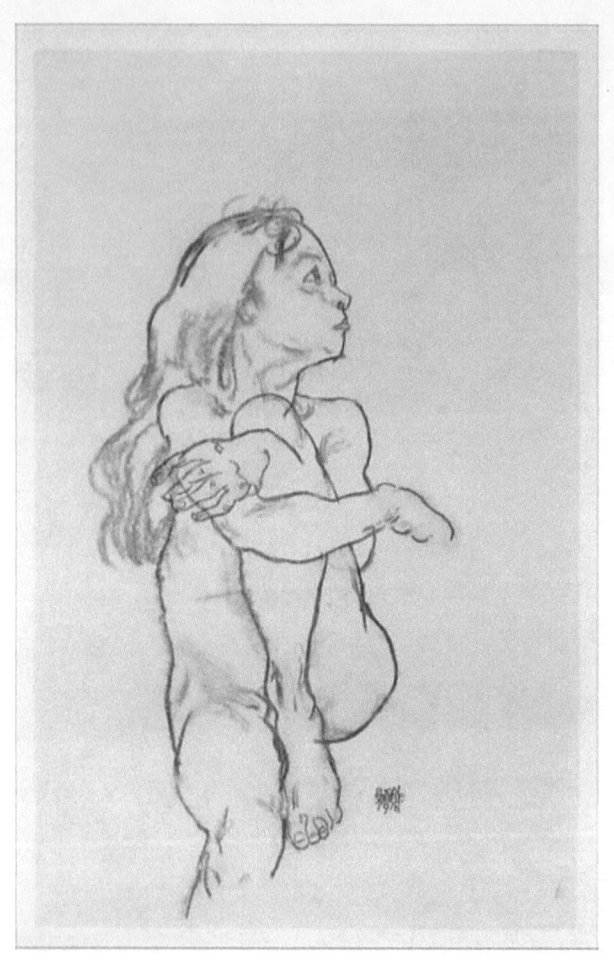

Seated Nude Girl Clasping Her Left Knee

1918, Charcoal on paper

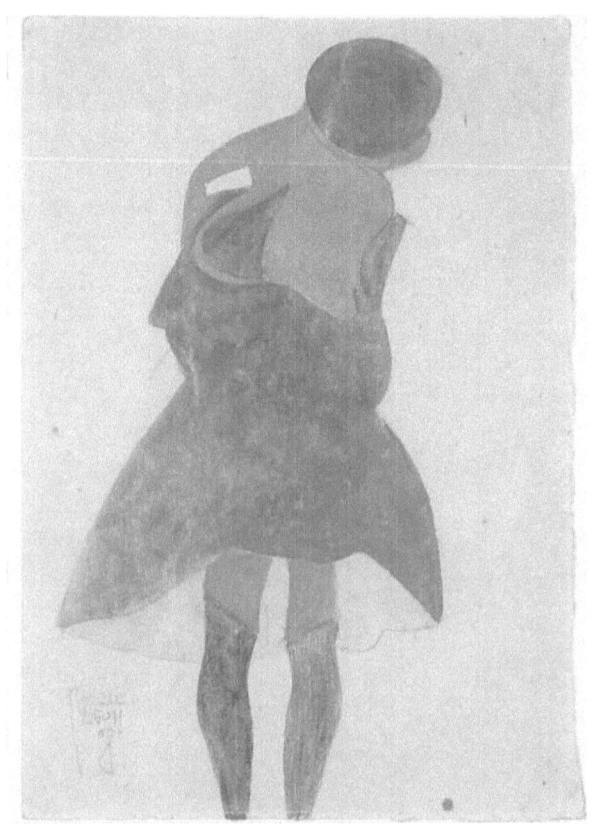

Standing Girl, Back View

1908, Gouache, watercolor, and graphite on paper

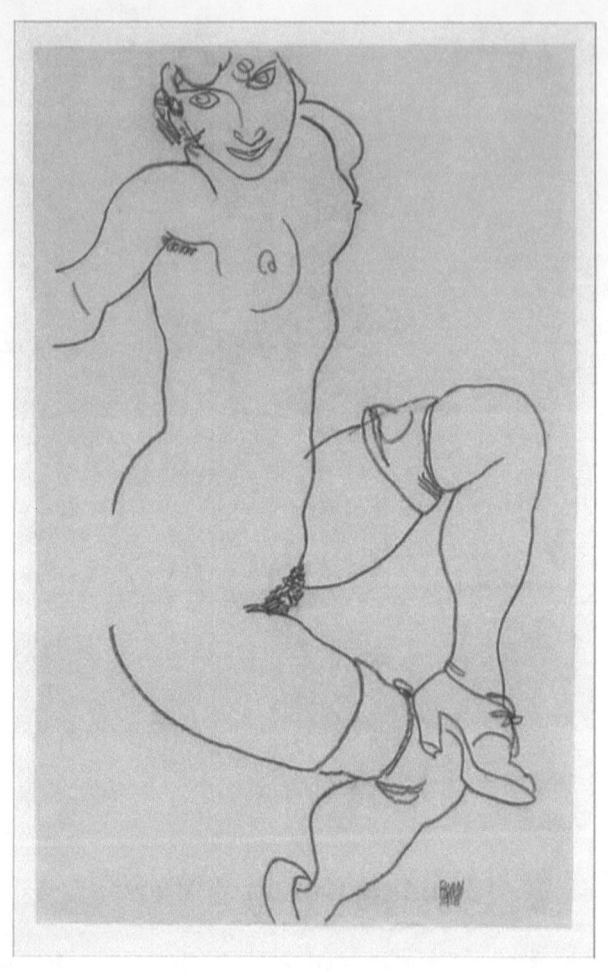

Seated Nude in Shoes and Stockings

1918, Charcoal on paper

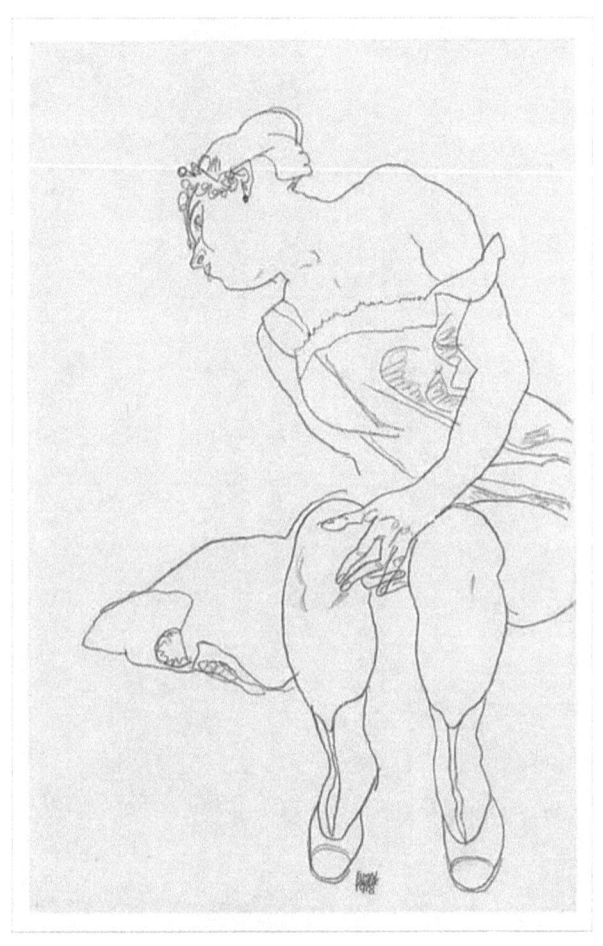

Seated Woman in Corset and Boots

1918, Crayon on paper

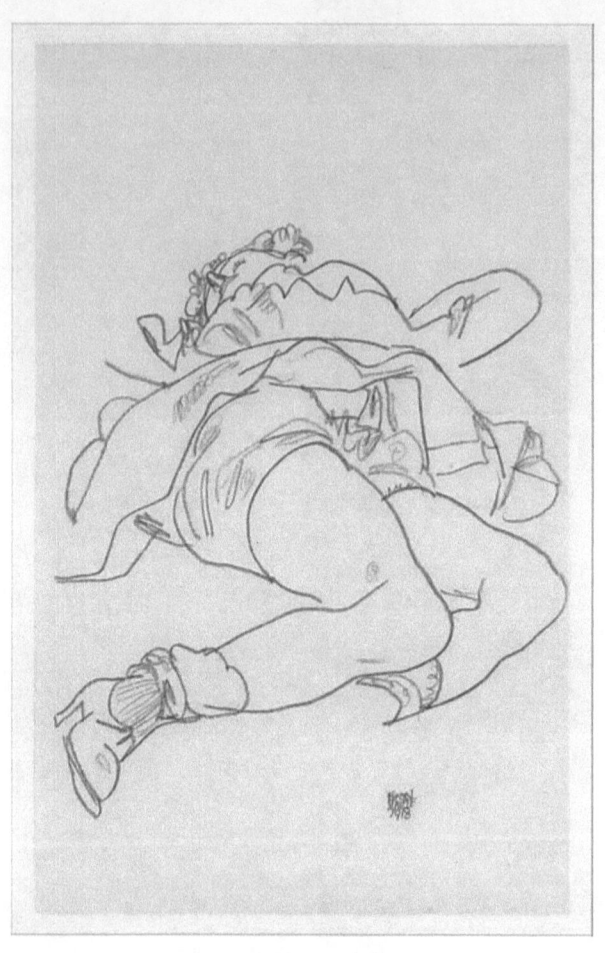

Reclining Woman with Raised Skirt

1918, Charcoal on paper

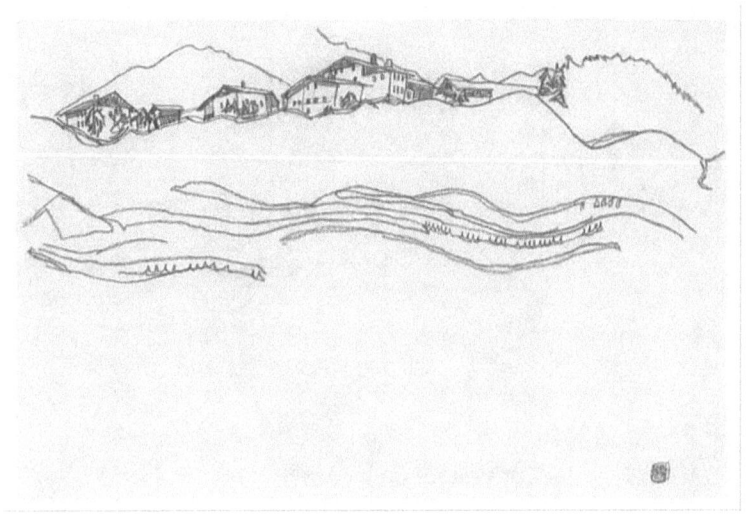

Landscape with Houses

1917, Charcoal on paper

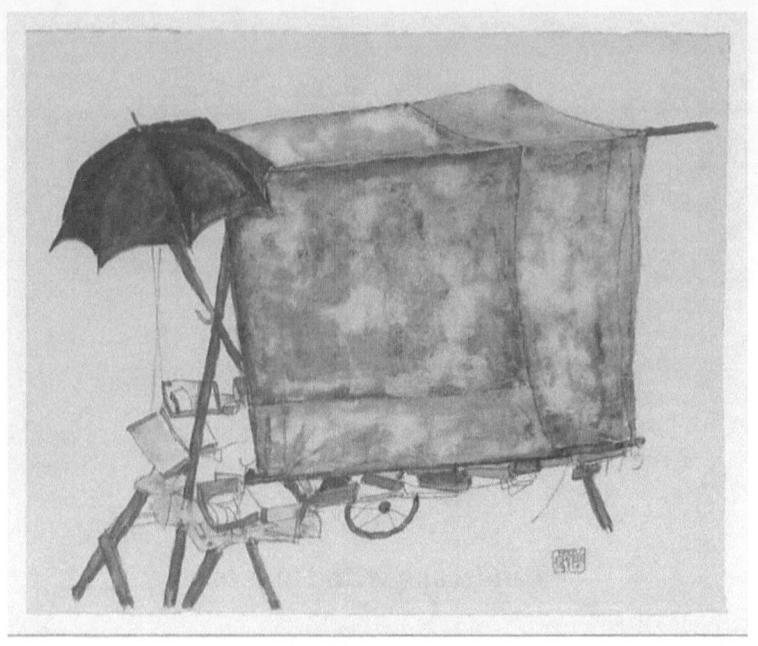

Street Cart

1914, Watercolor, gouache, and graphite on paper

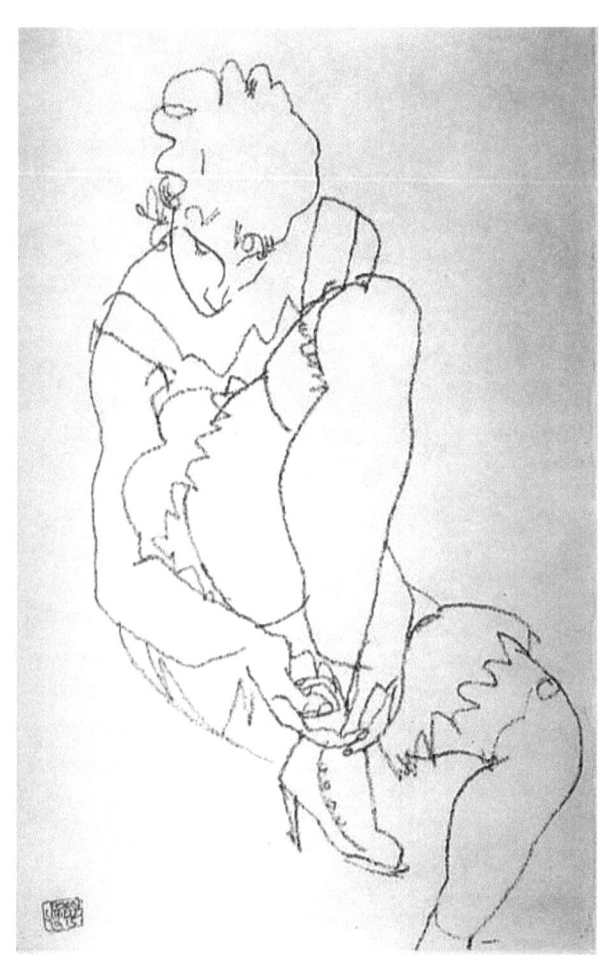

Woman Buttoning Her Shoes

1915, Charcoal on paper

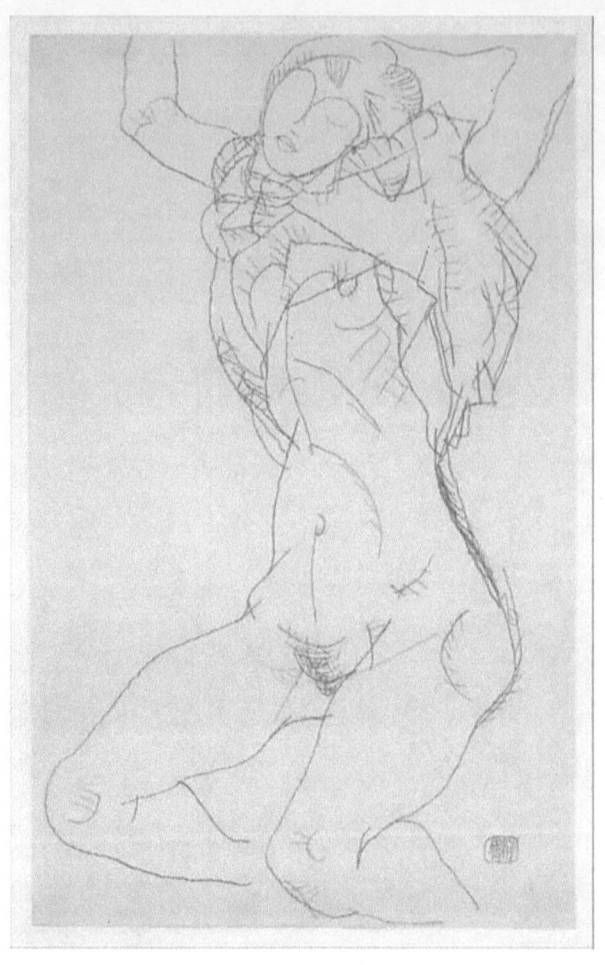

Reclining Semi-Nude with Arms Raised

1914, Graphite on paper

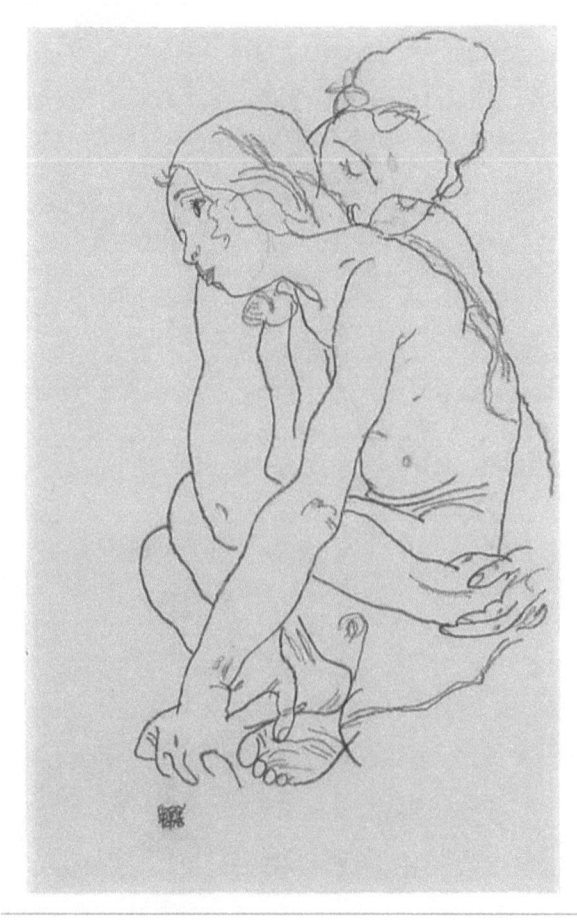

Two Women Embracing

1918, Charcoal on paper

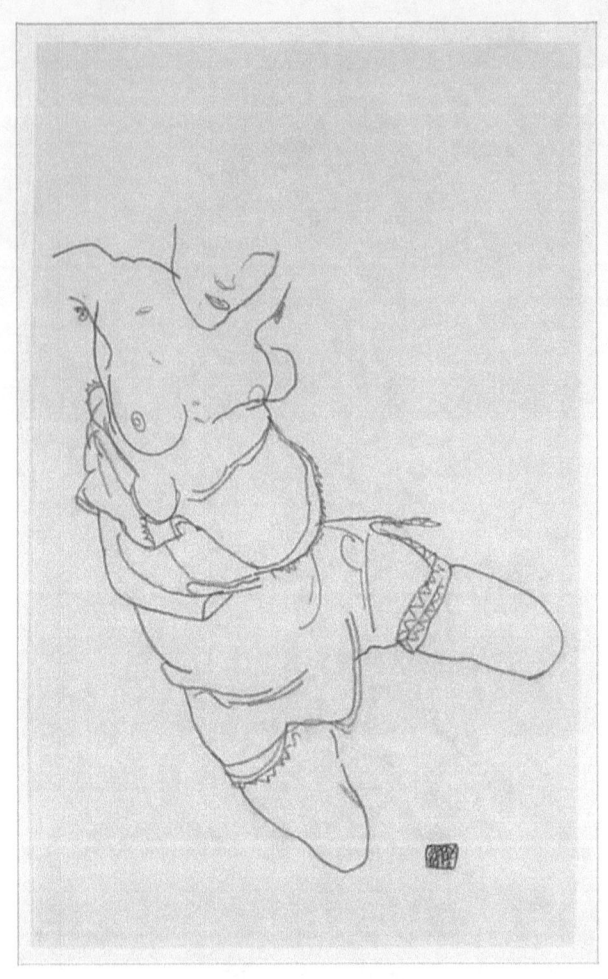

Semi-Dressed Model

1917, Charcoal on paper

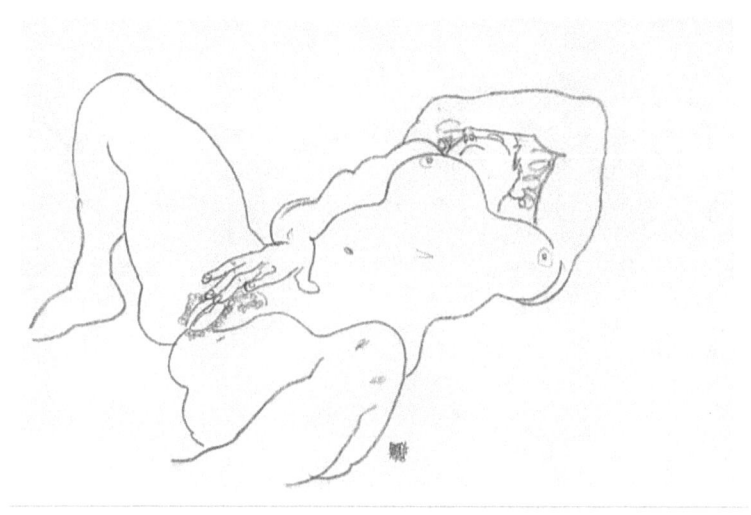

Reclining Nude

1918, Crayon on paper

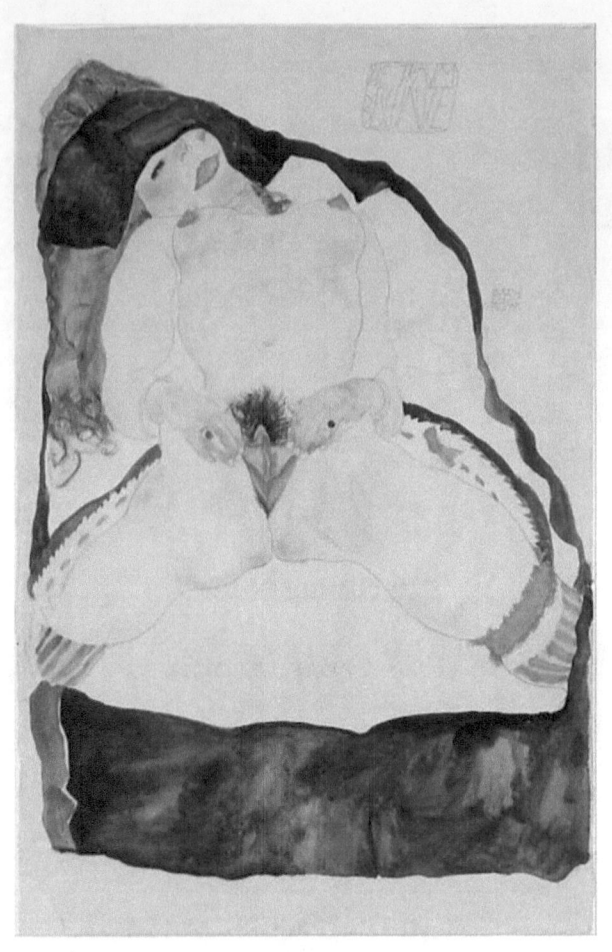

Girl Seen in a Dream

1911, Watercolor and graphite on paper

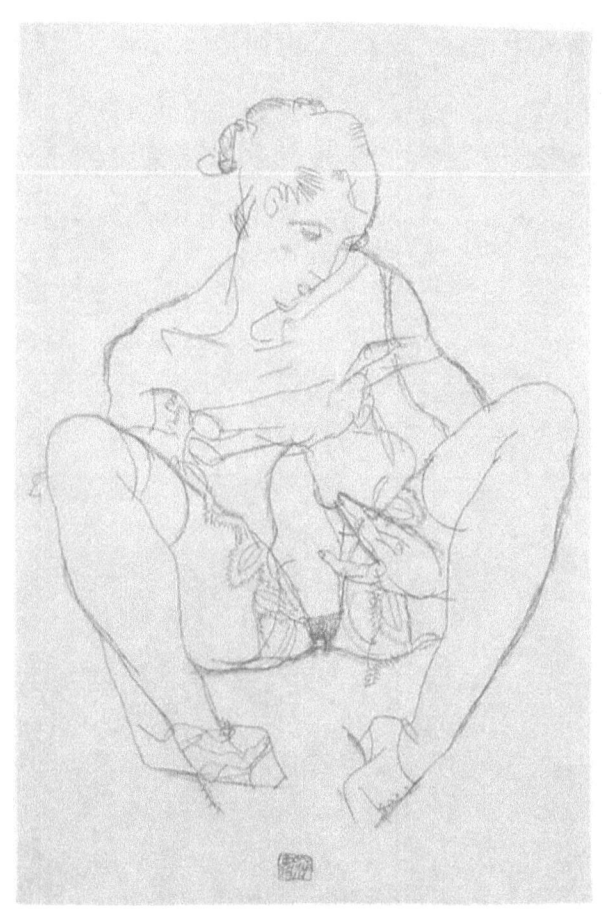

Seated Woman in Chemise

1914, Graphite on paper

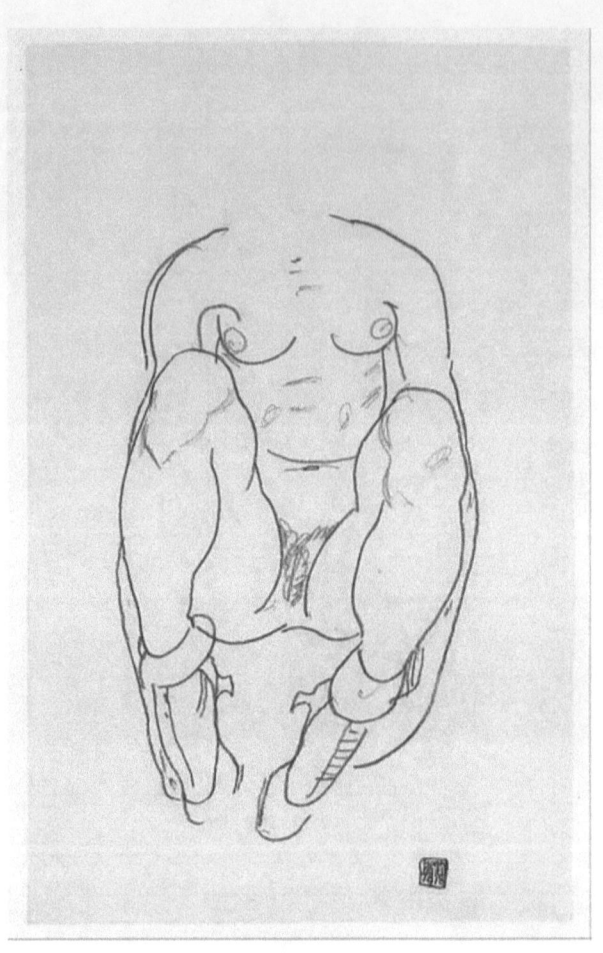

Torso of a Seated Woman with Boots

1918, Charcoal on paper

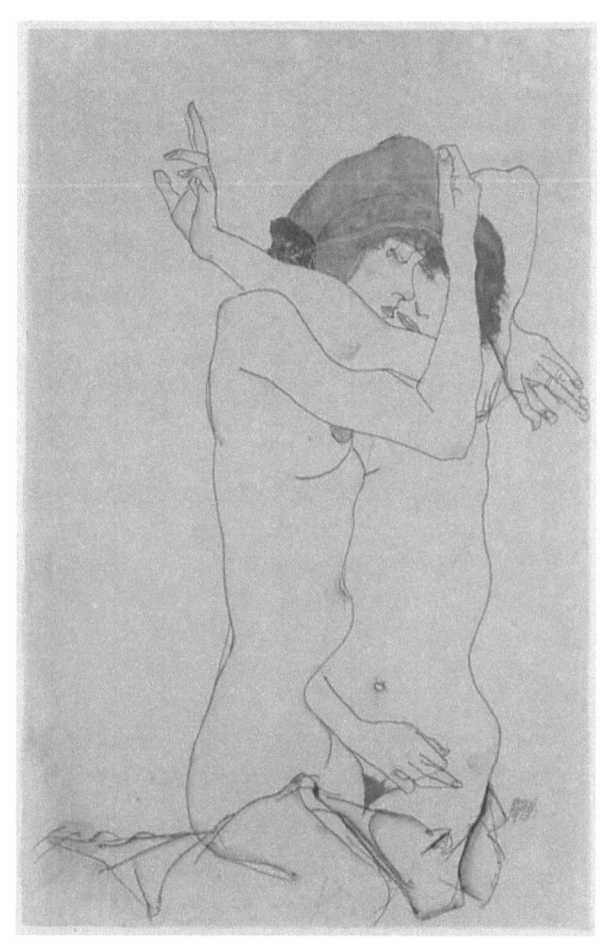

Two Women Embracing

1913, Gouache, watercolor, and graphite on paper

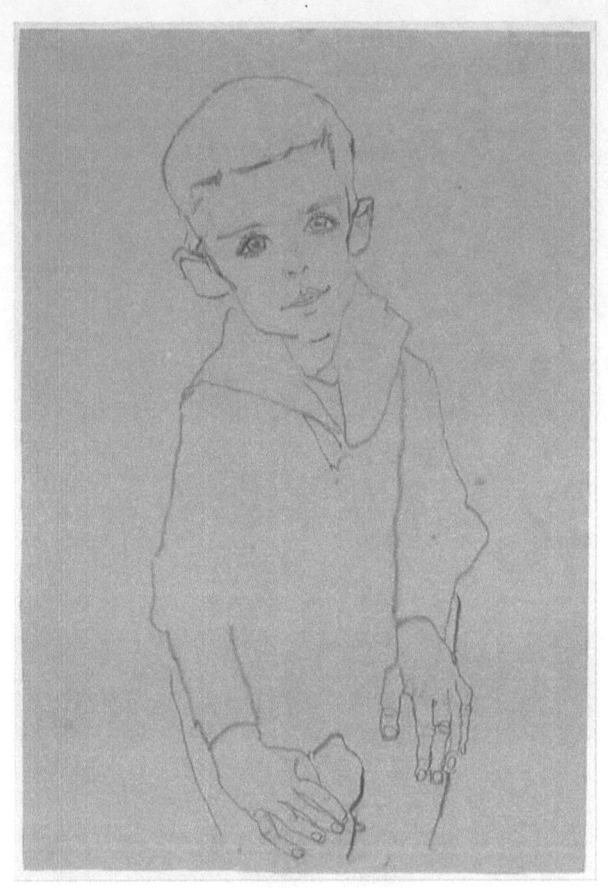

Portrait of Herbert Rainer

1910, Graphite on paper

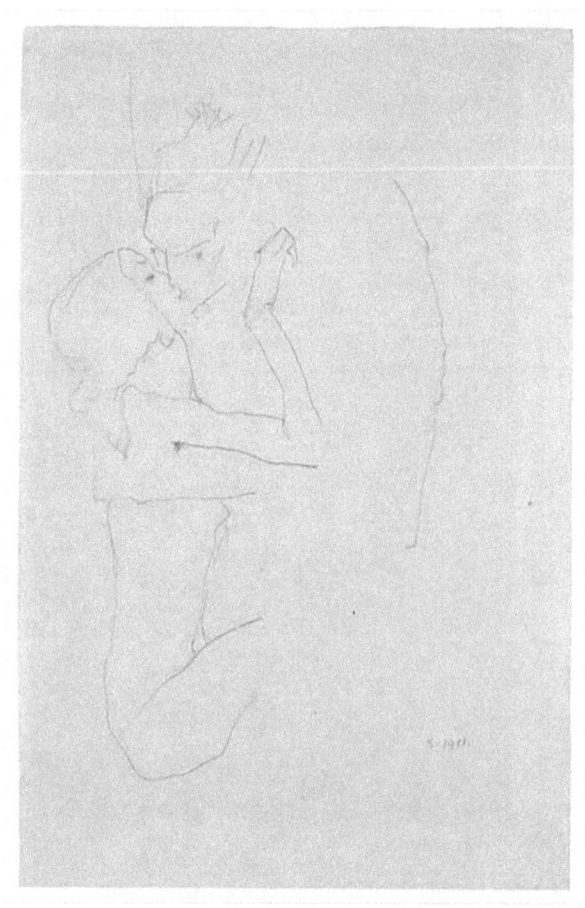

The Kiss

1911, Graphite on paper

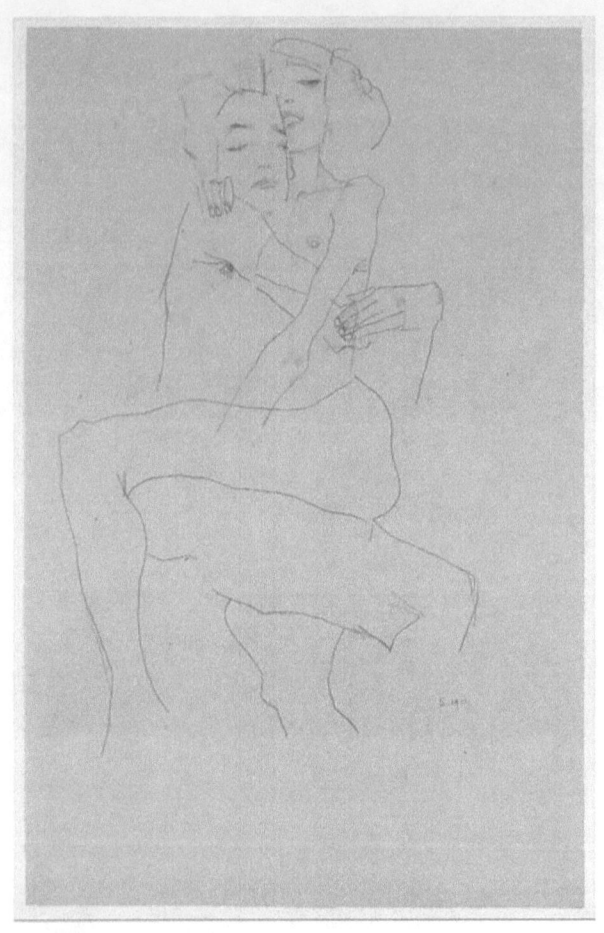

Couple Embracing

1911, Graphite on paper

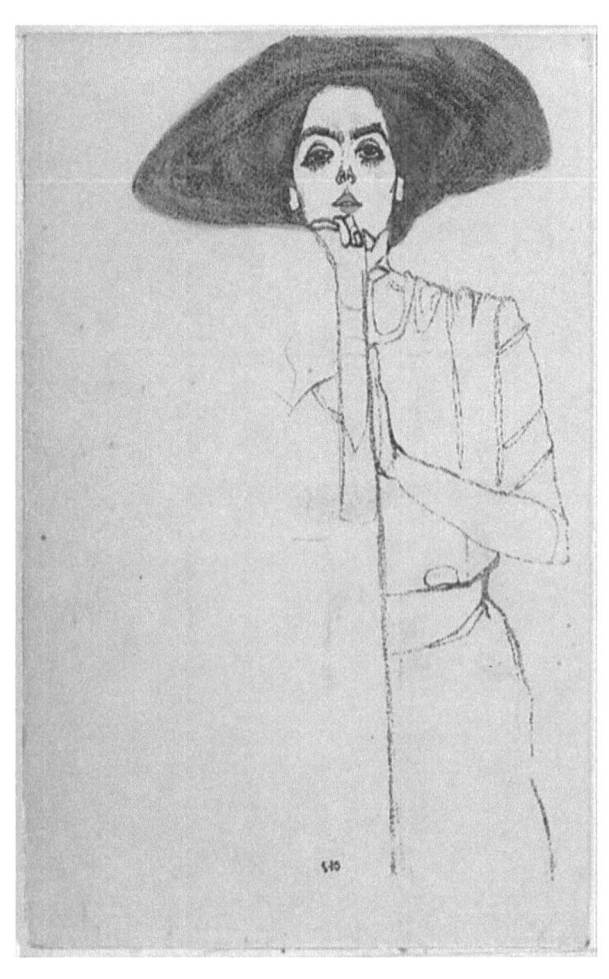

Portrait of a Woman

1910, Color lithograph

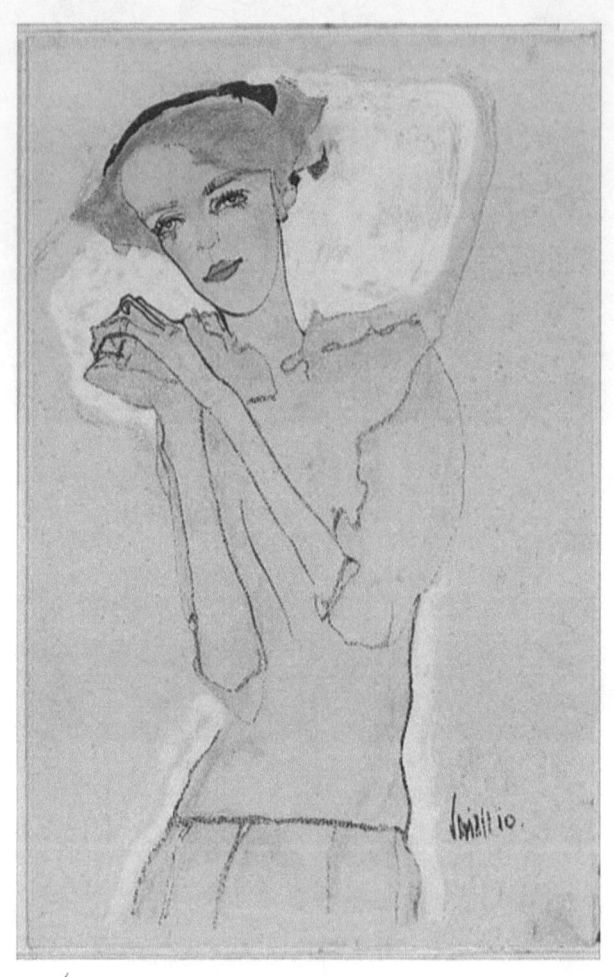

Portrait of a Woman

1910, Color lithograph

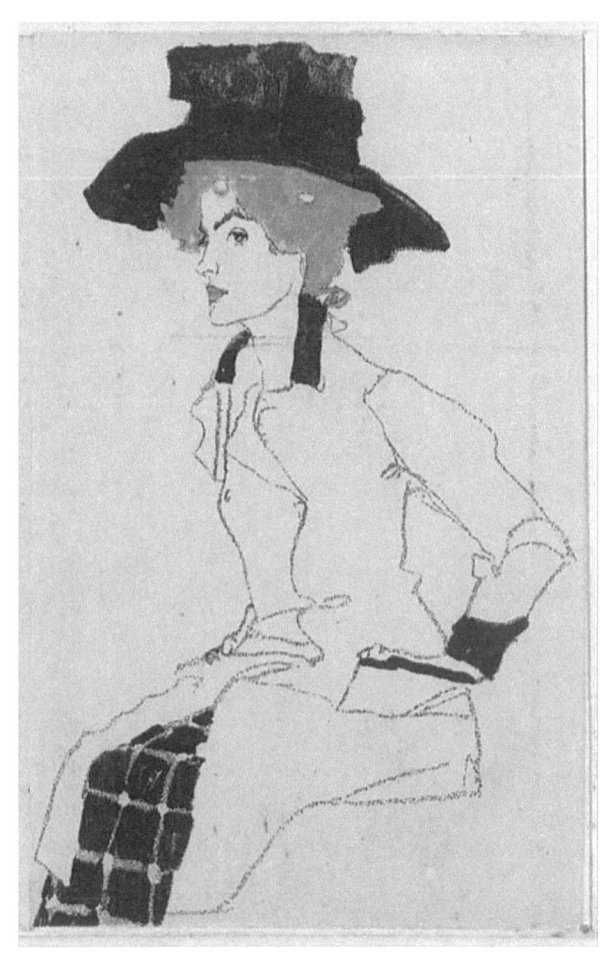

Portrait of a Woman

1910, Color lithograph

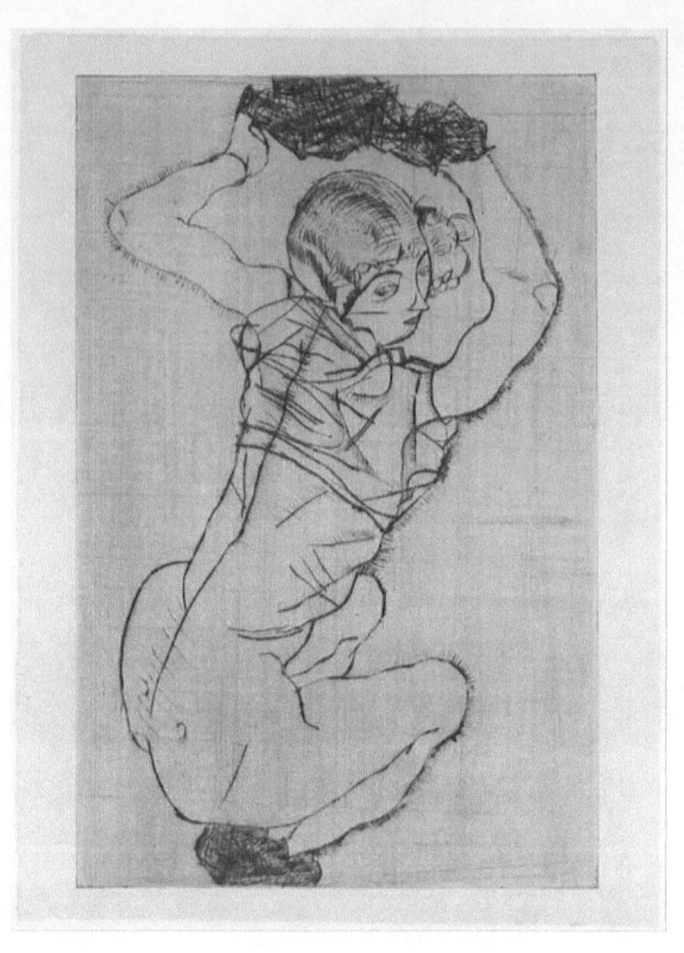

Squatting Woman

1914, Drypoint

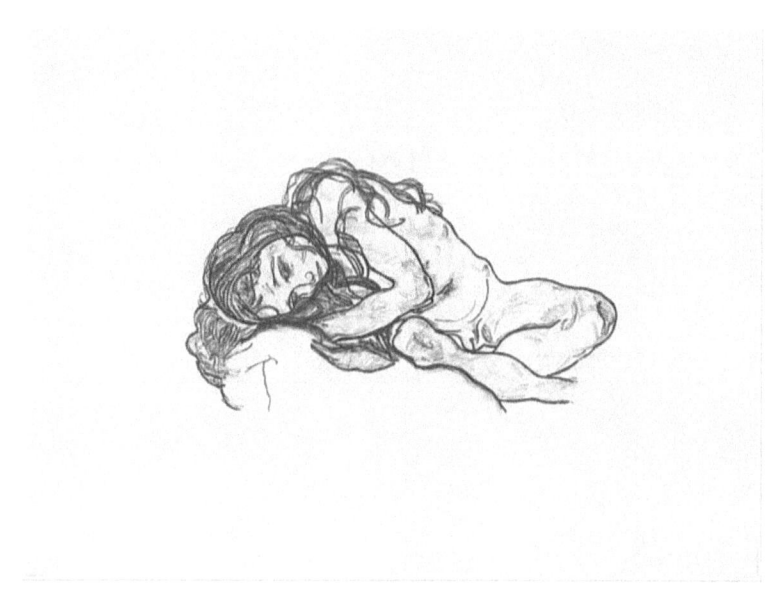

Girl

1918, Lithograph

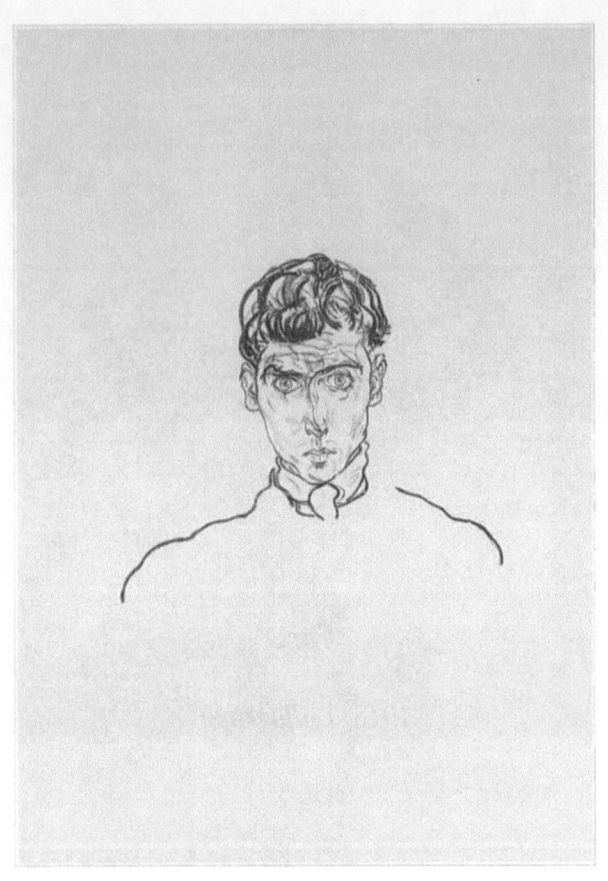

Portrait of Paris von Gütersloh

1918, Lithograph

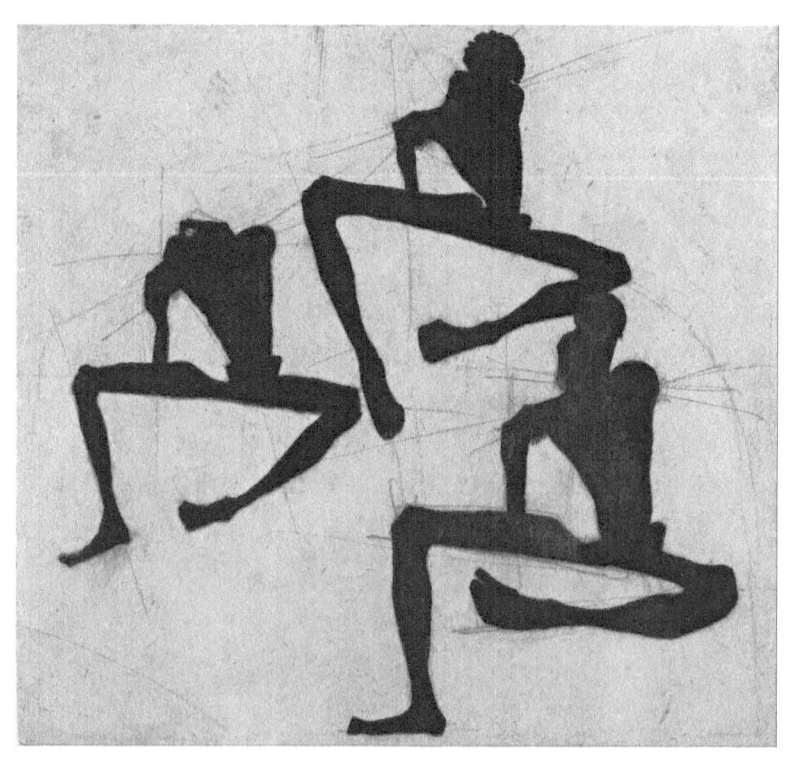

Composition with Three Male Nudes, 1910

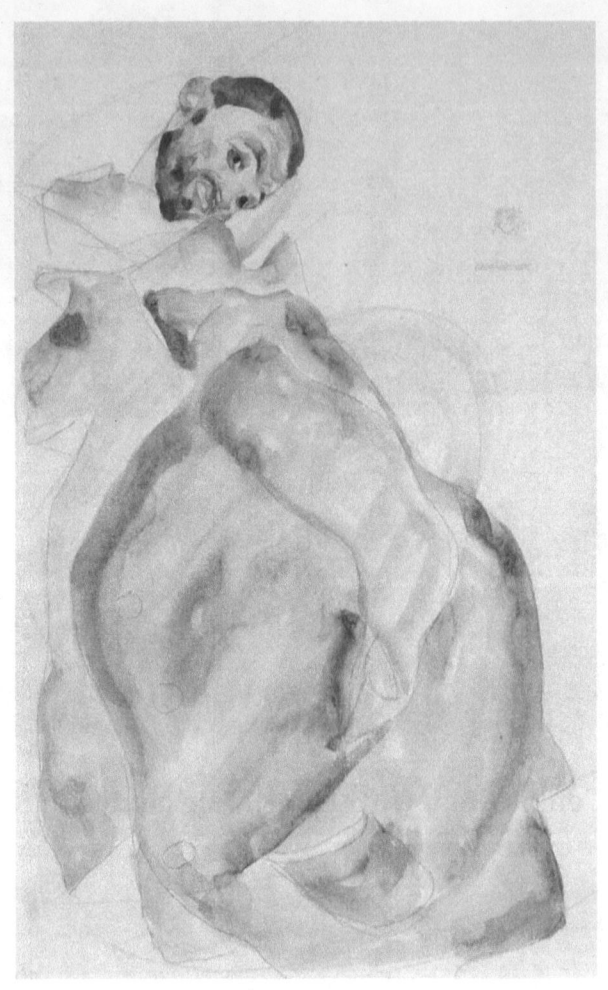

Prisoner, 1912

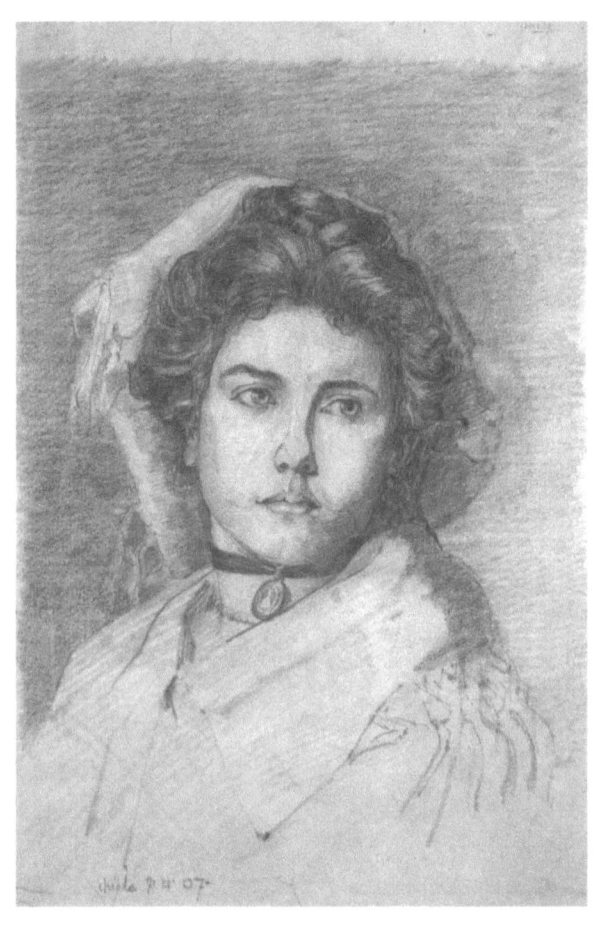

**Portrait of a woman with a collar and a medallion,
1907**

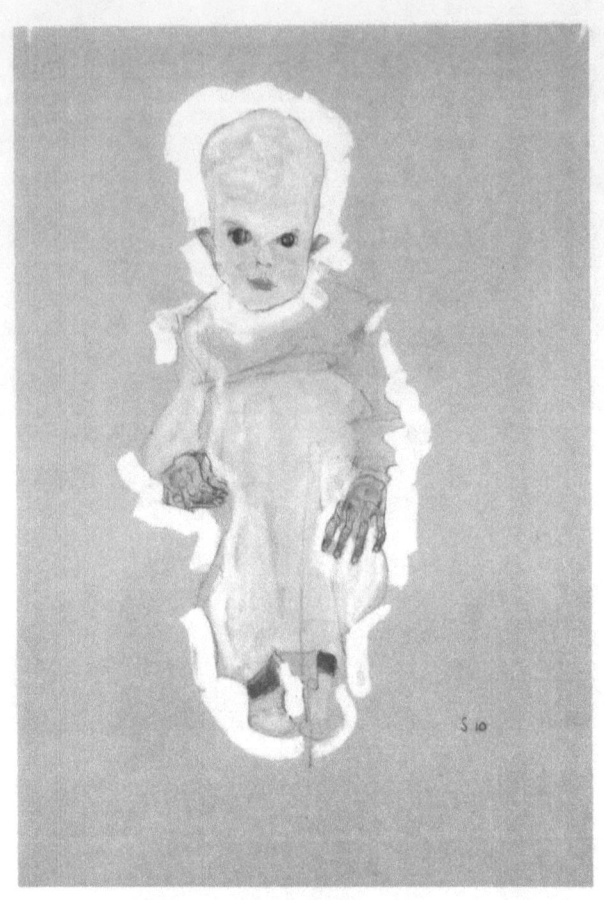

Baby, 1910

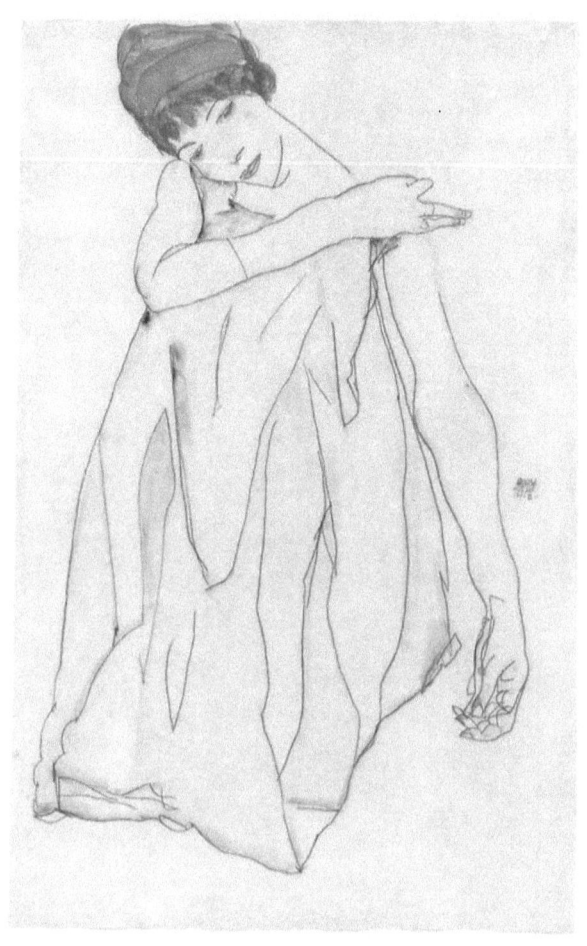

Dancer 1913

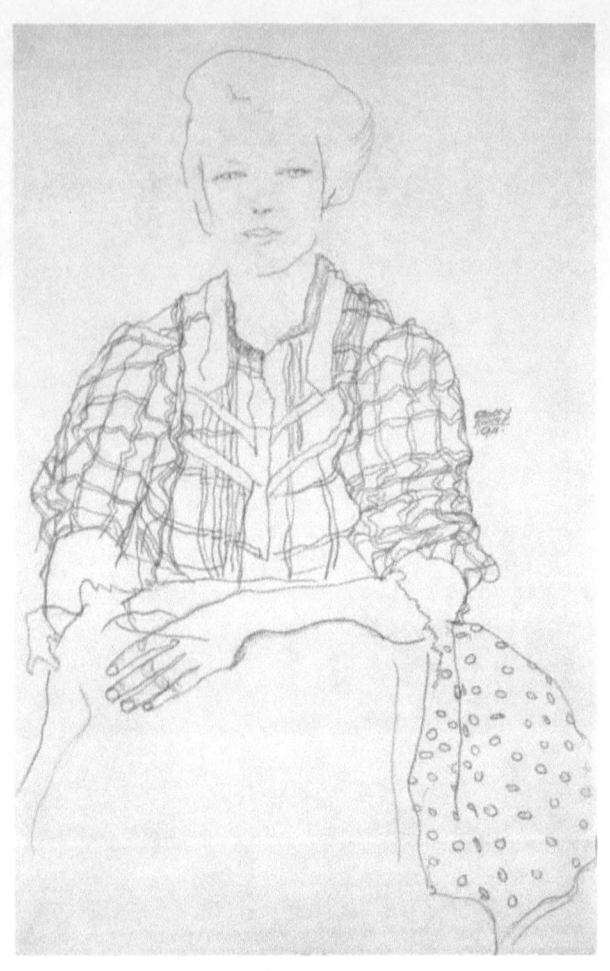

Girl in a plaid shirt, 1911

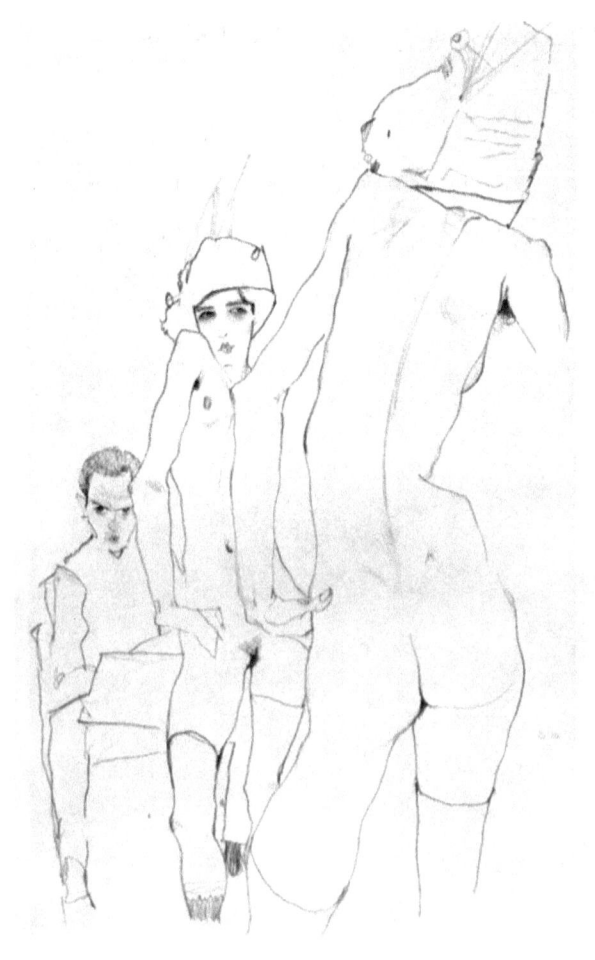

Drawing a Model in front of a Mirror, 1910

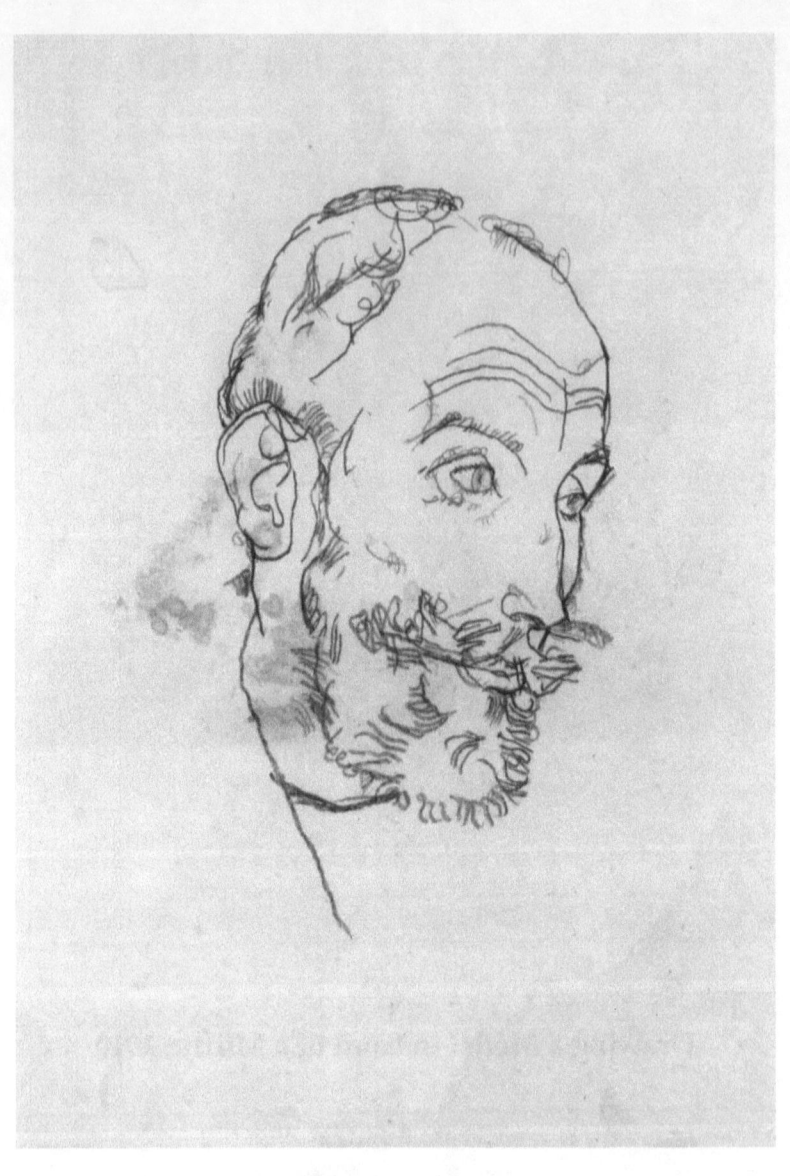

Franz Hauer,1914

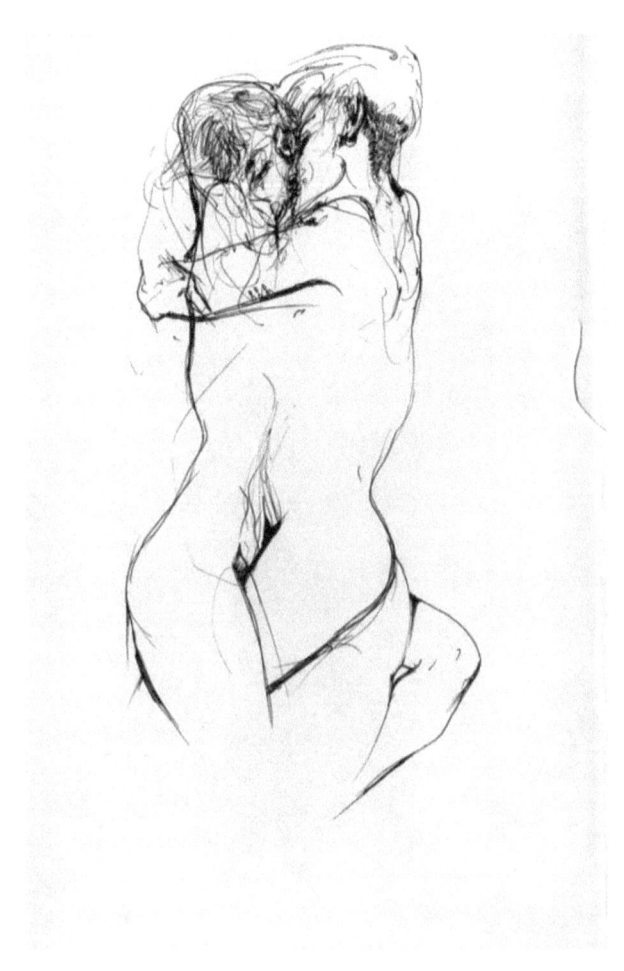

Embracing Couple, n.d.

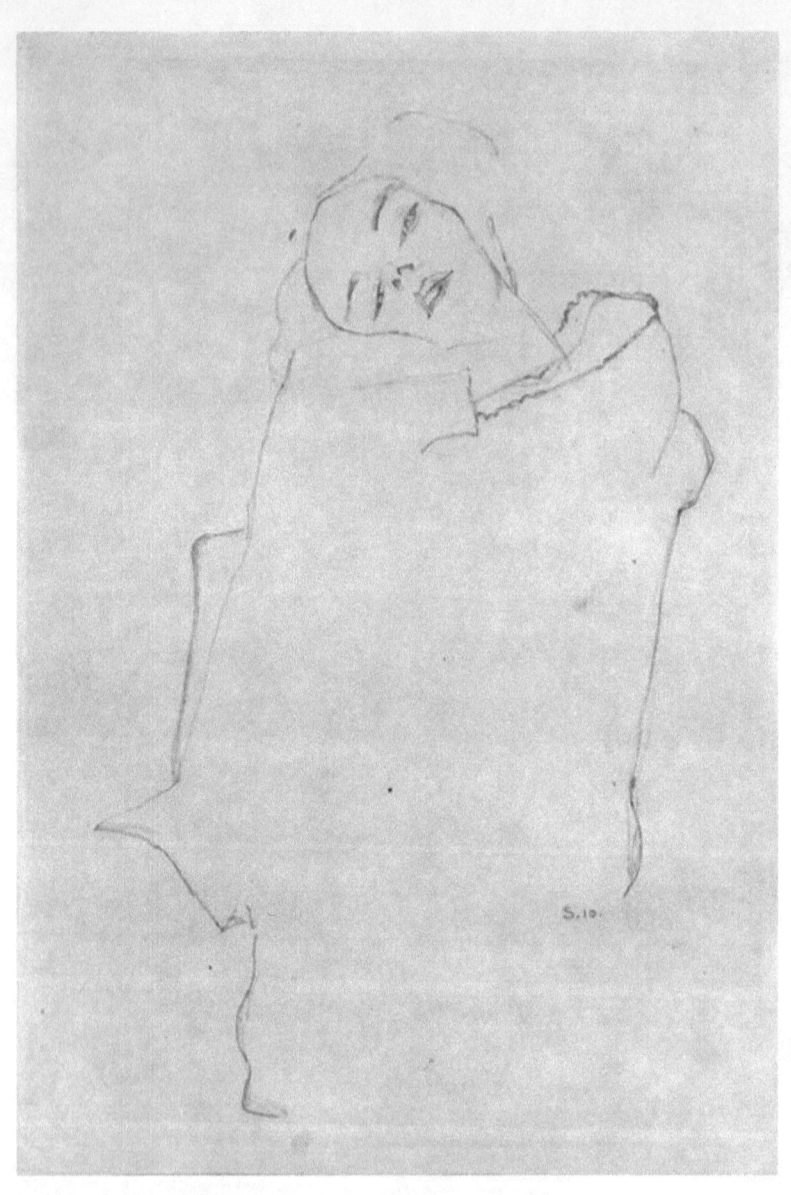

Girl with Head Tilted, 1910

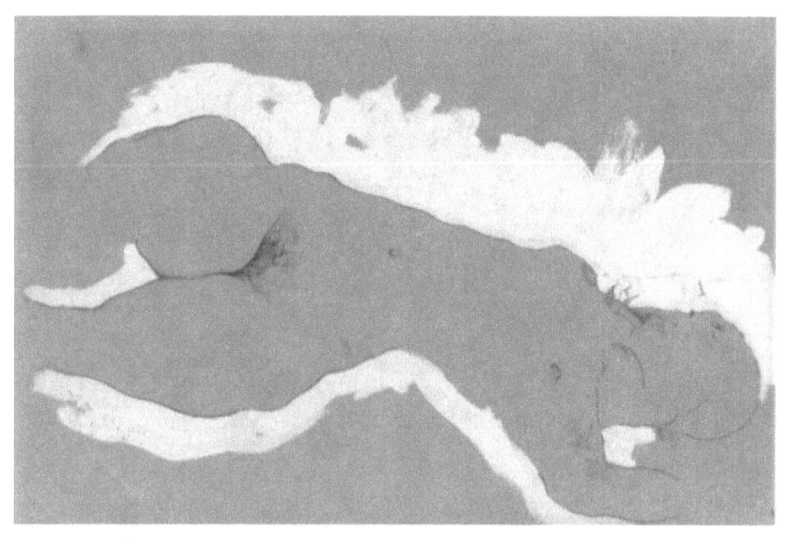

Female nude with white border

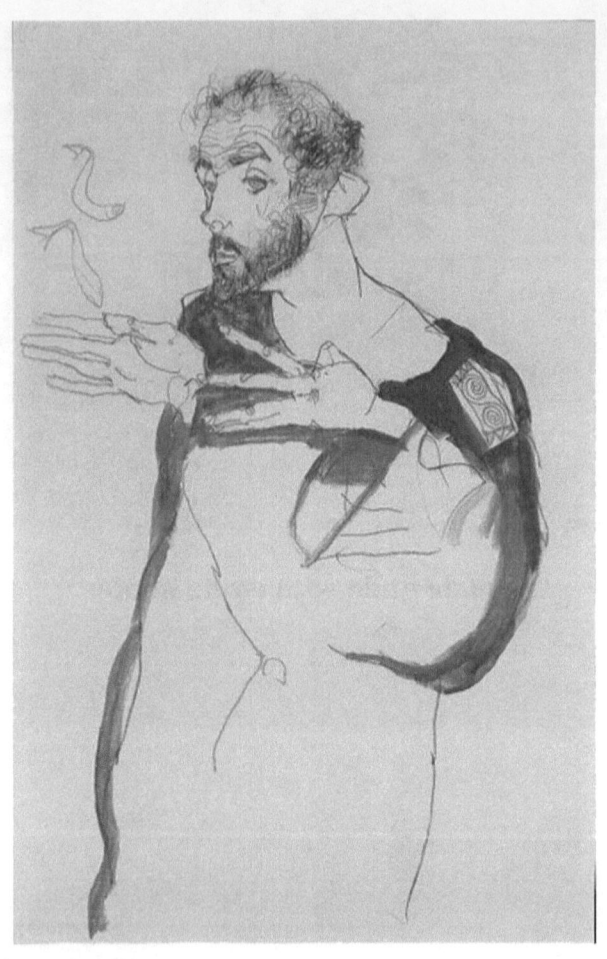

Gustav Klimt in his Blue Painting Smock, 1913

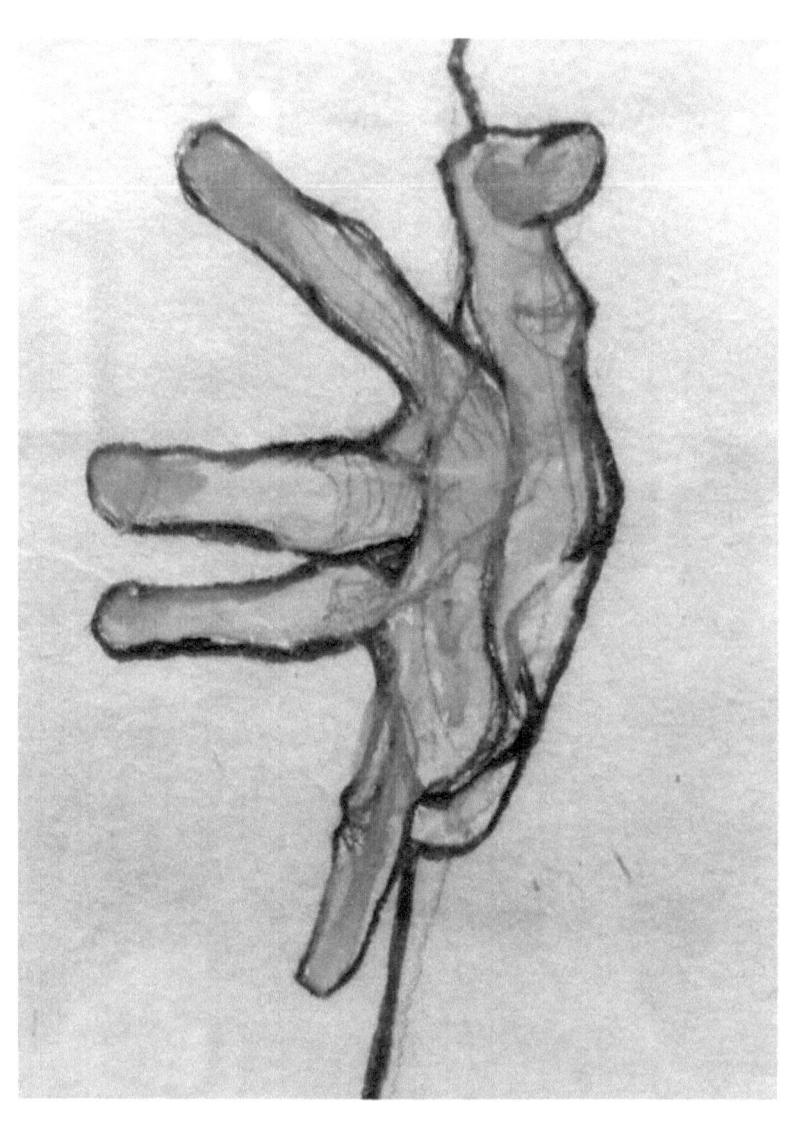

Hand Study, 1912

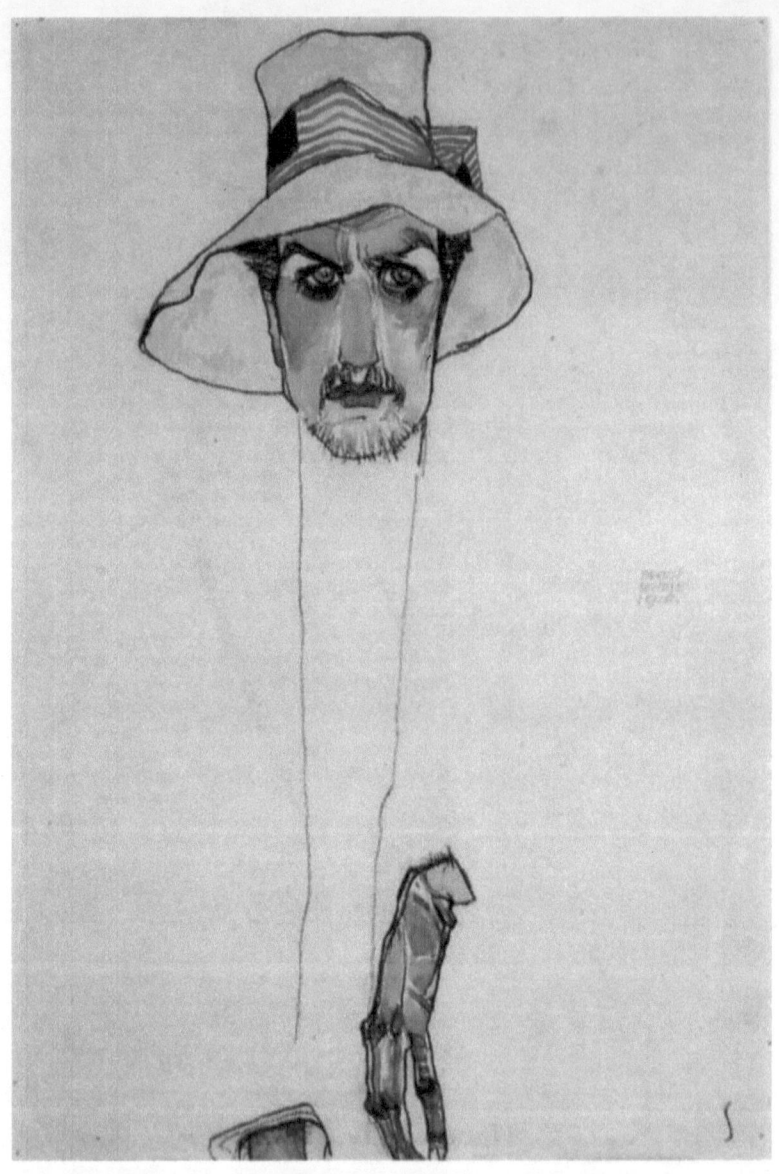

Portrait of a Man with a Floppy Hat (Portrait of Erwin Dominilk Osen), 1910

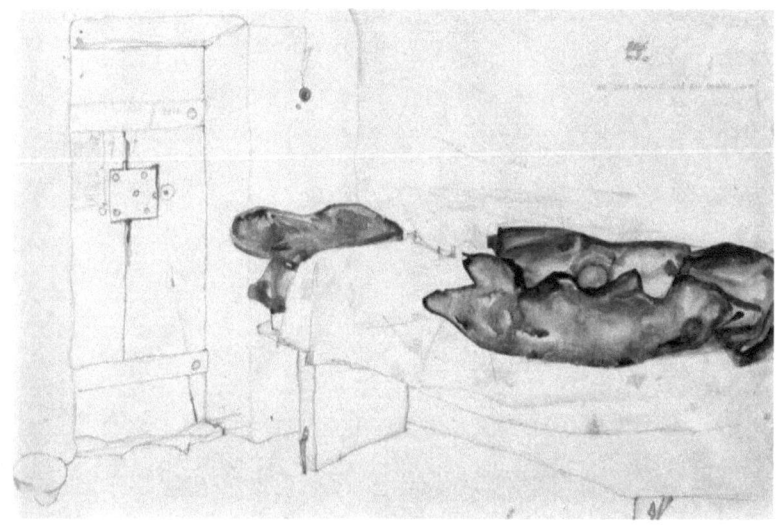

Prison

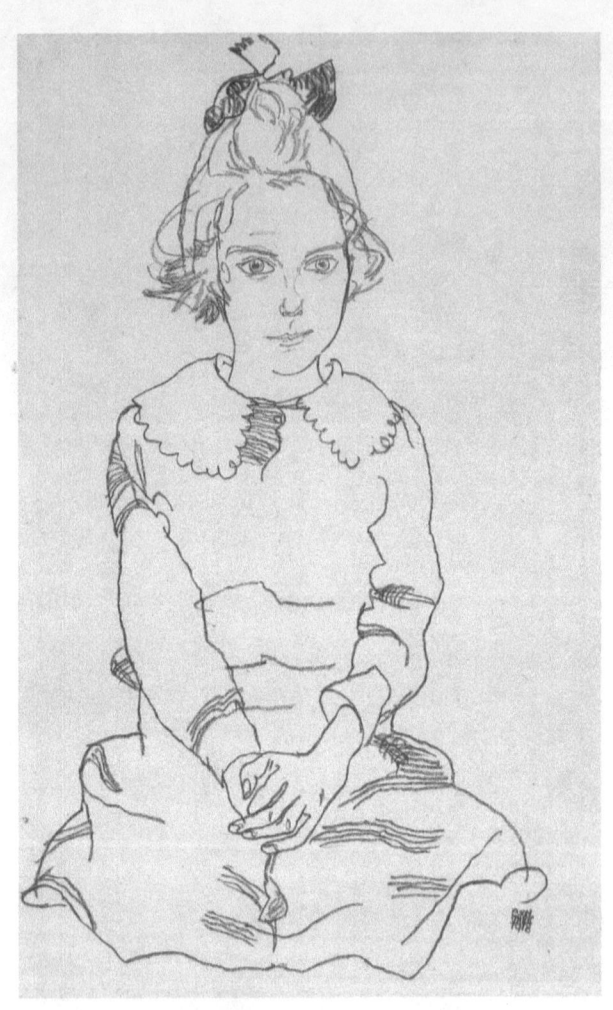

Portrait of Maria Steiner, 1918

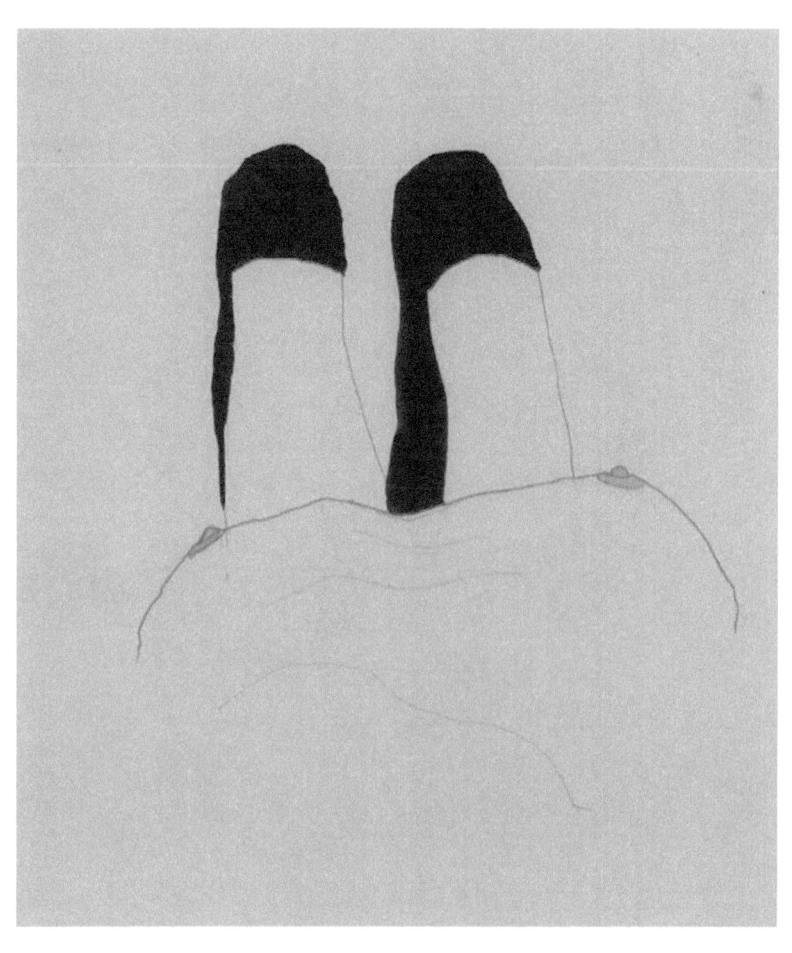

Black Stockings

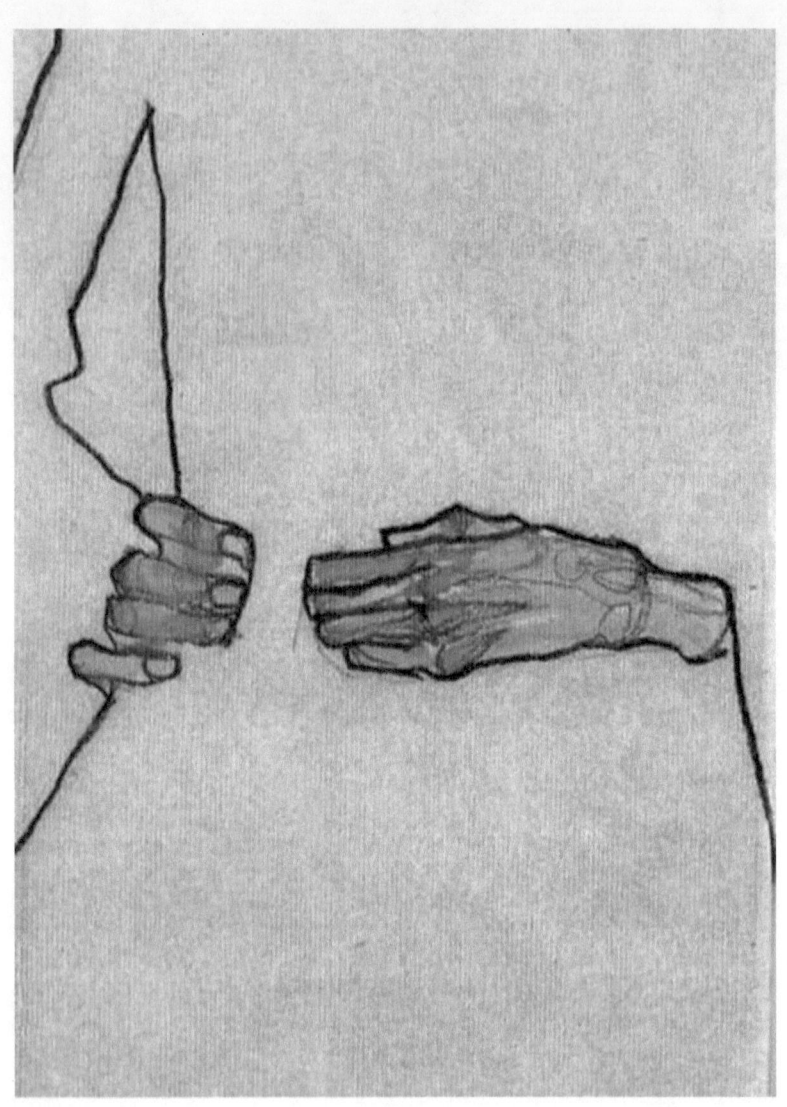

Hands

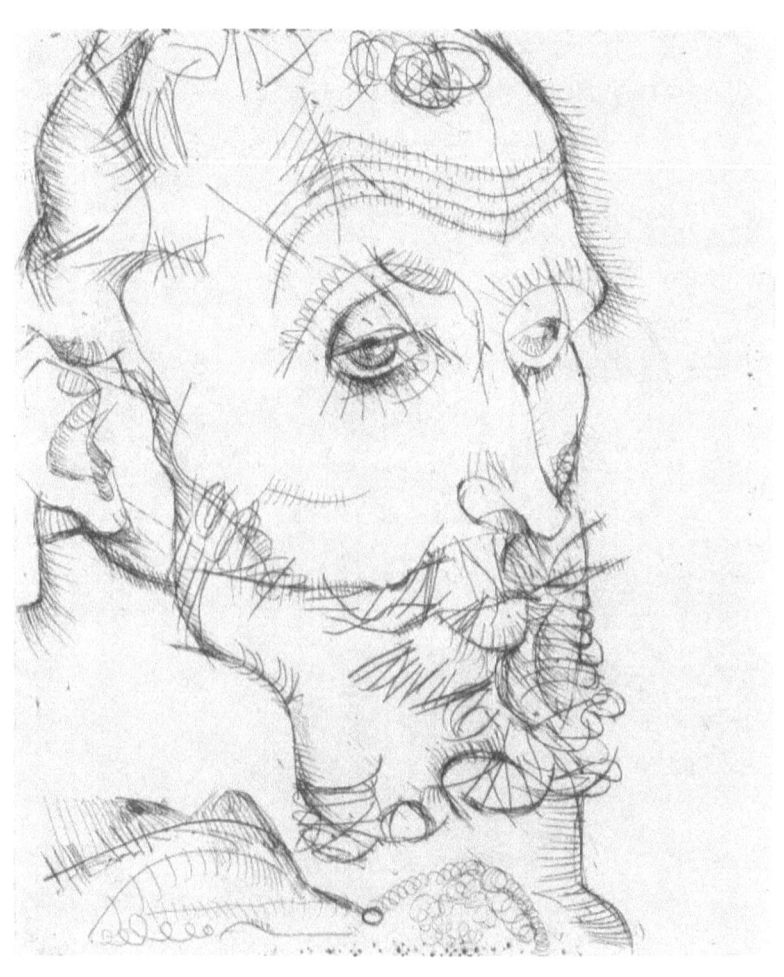

Portrait of Franz Hauer, 1914

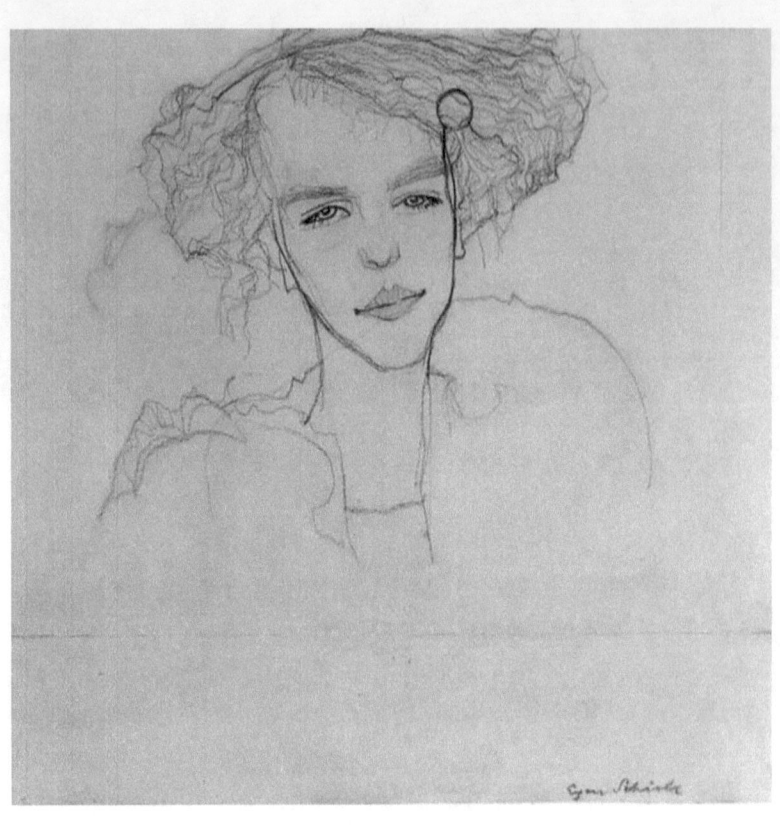

Portrait of Girl

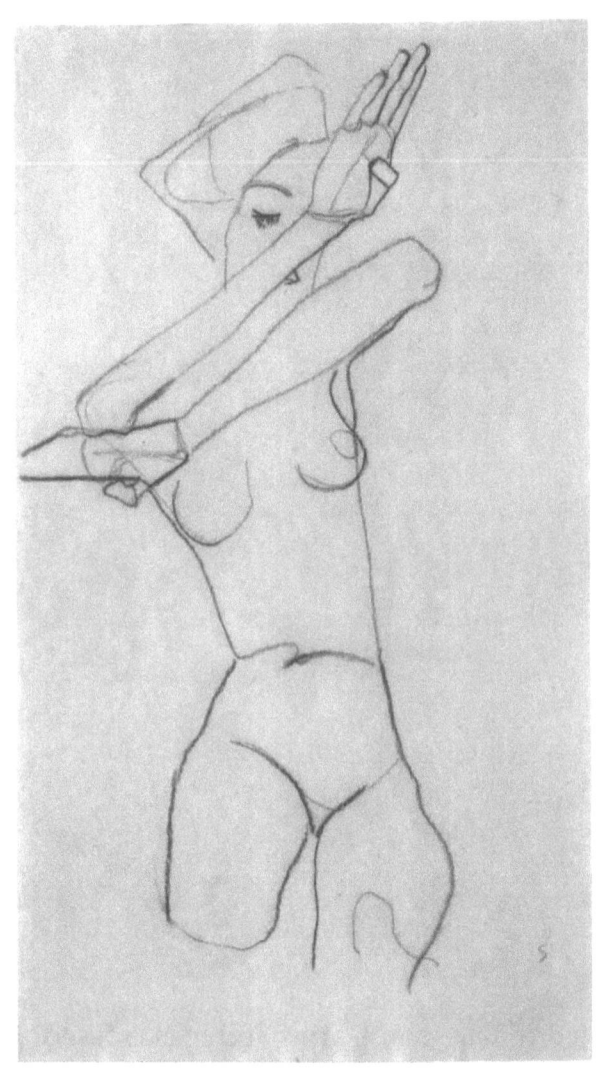

Seated female nude with raised arms

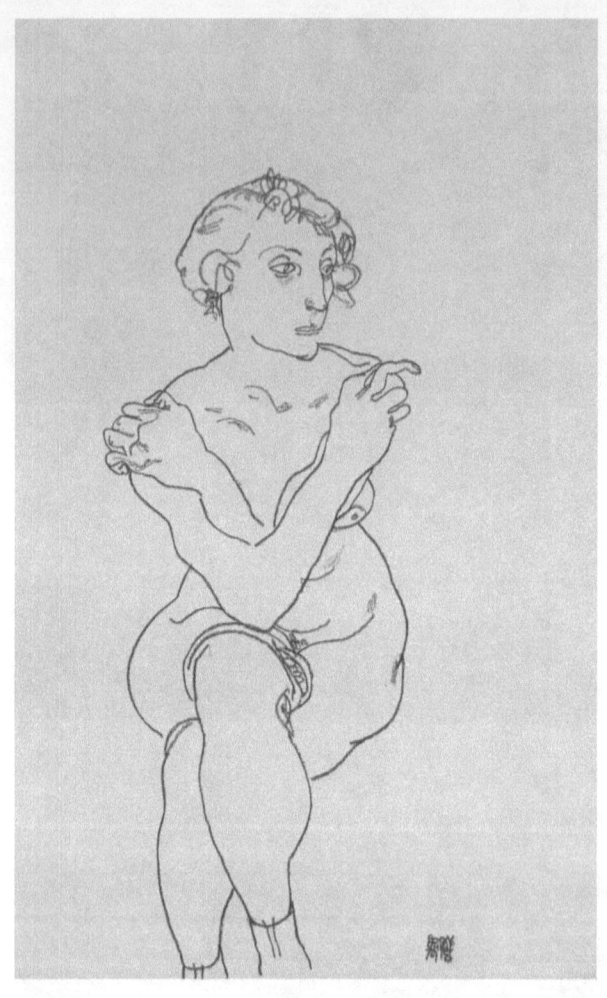

Seated female nude, arms and legs crossed, 1918

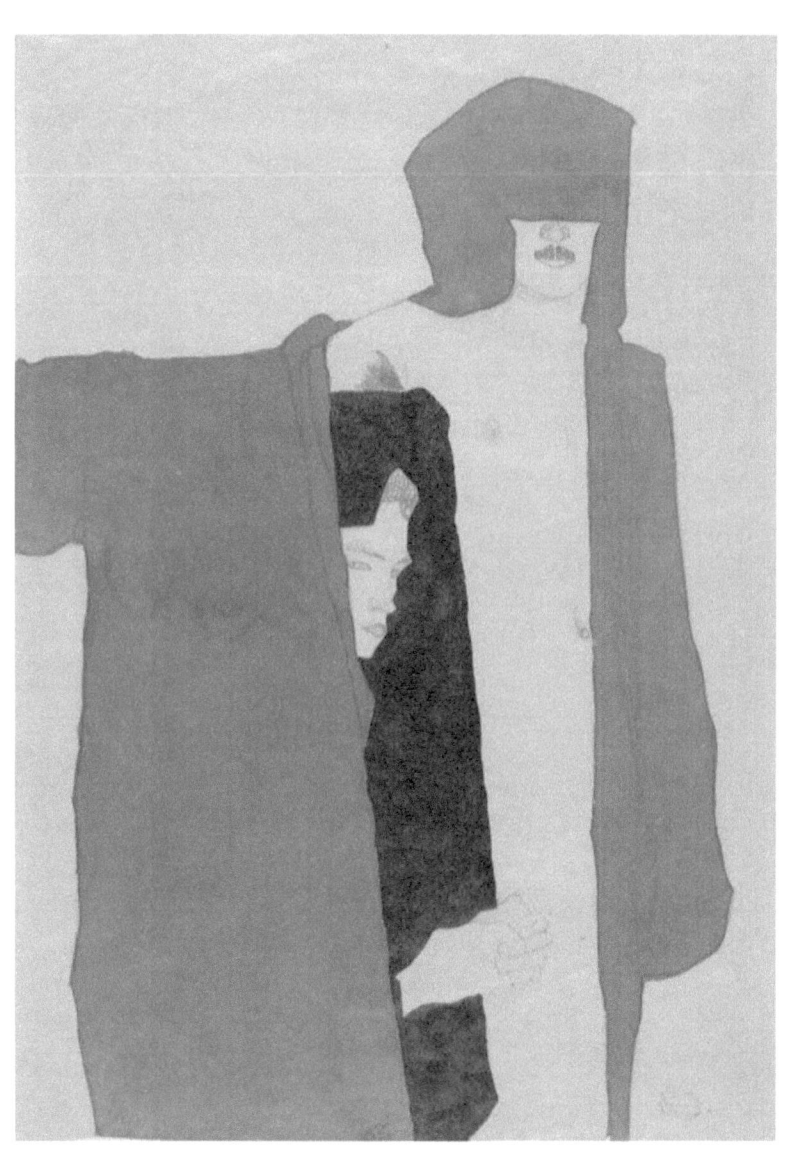

The Couple, 1909

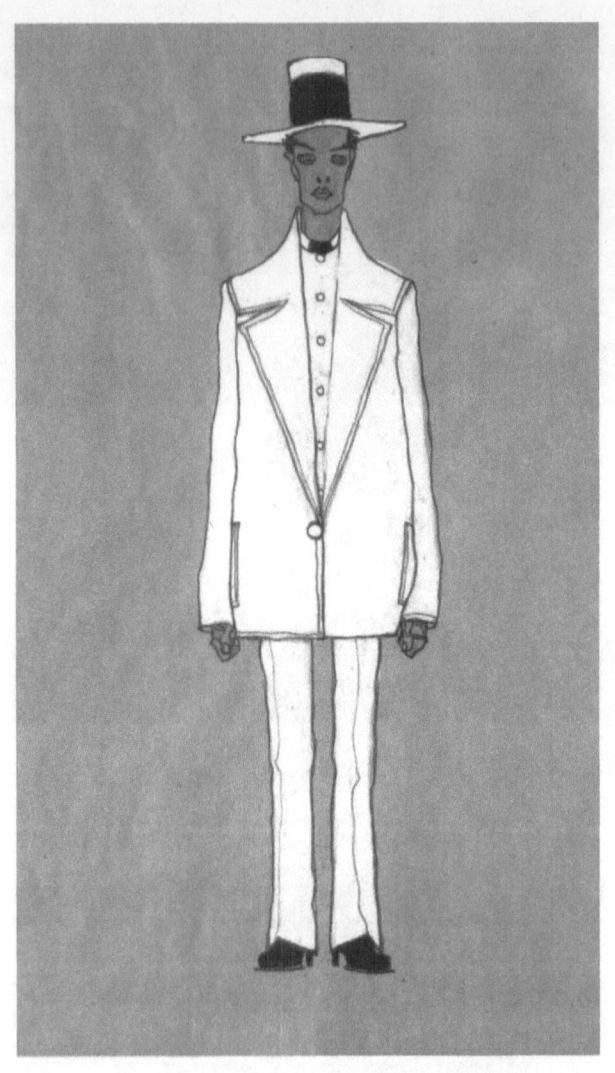

Self-portrait with white suit

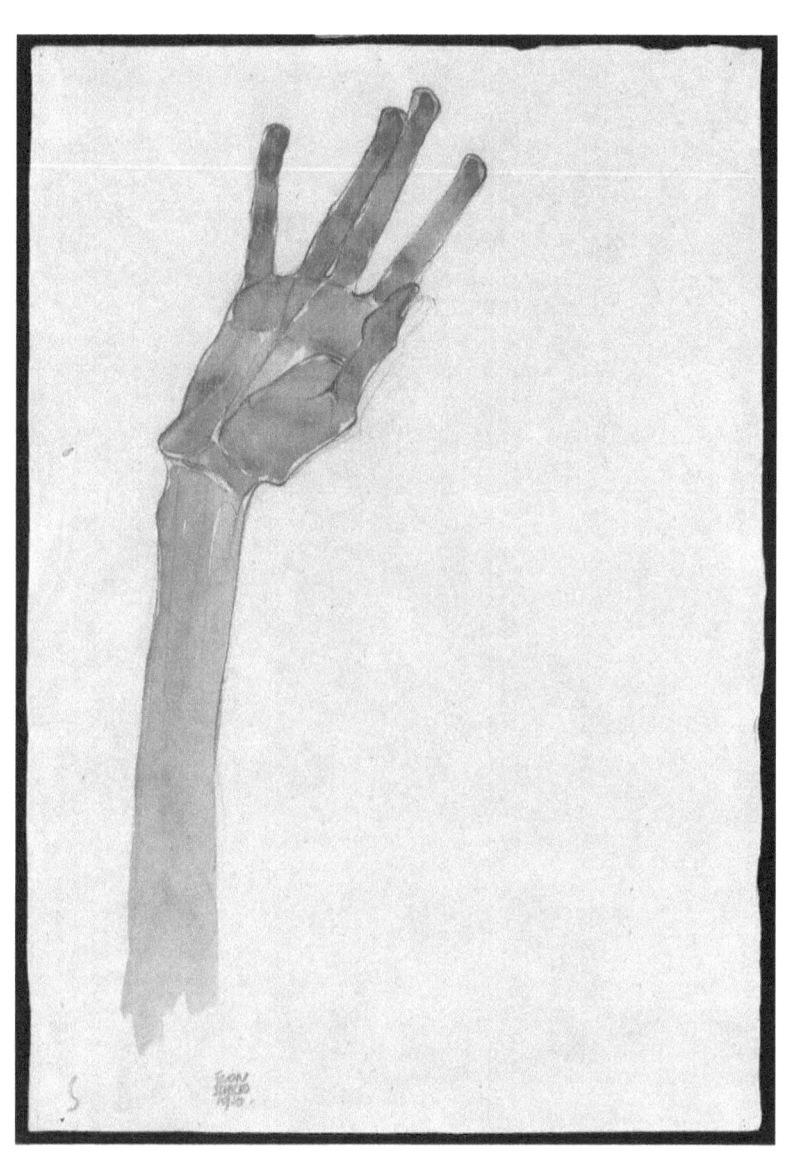

The Red Hand

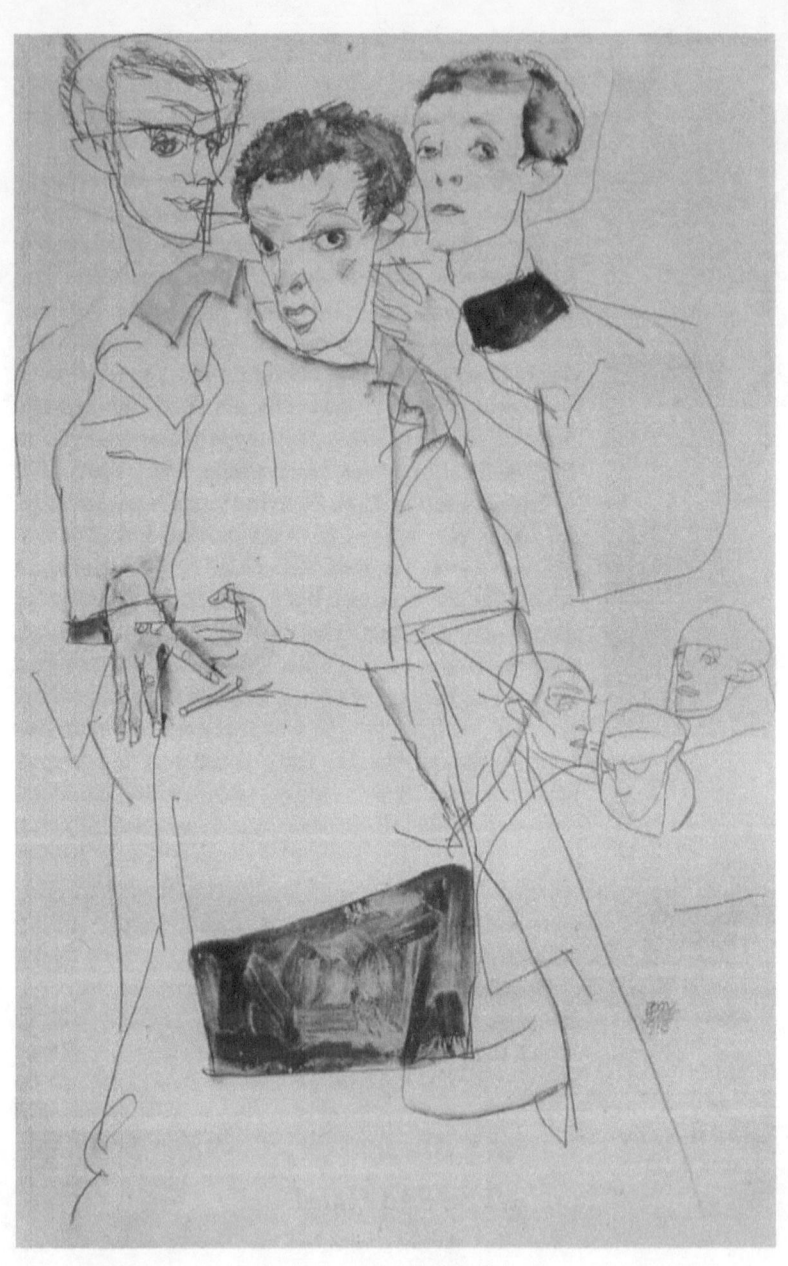

Triple Self Portrait, 1913

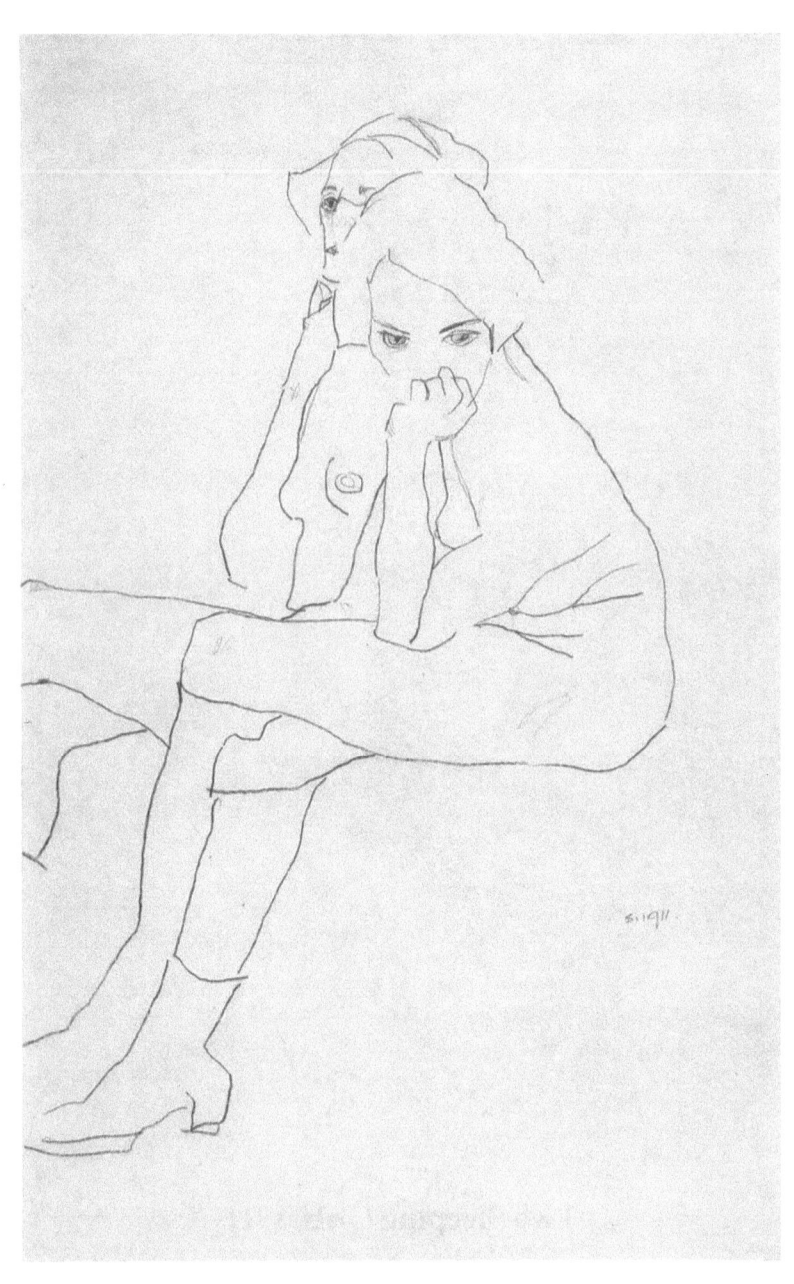

Two Seated Girls, 1911

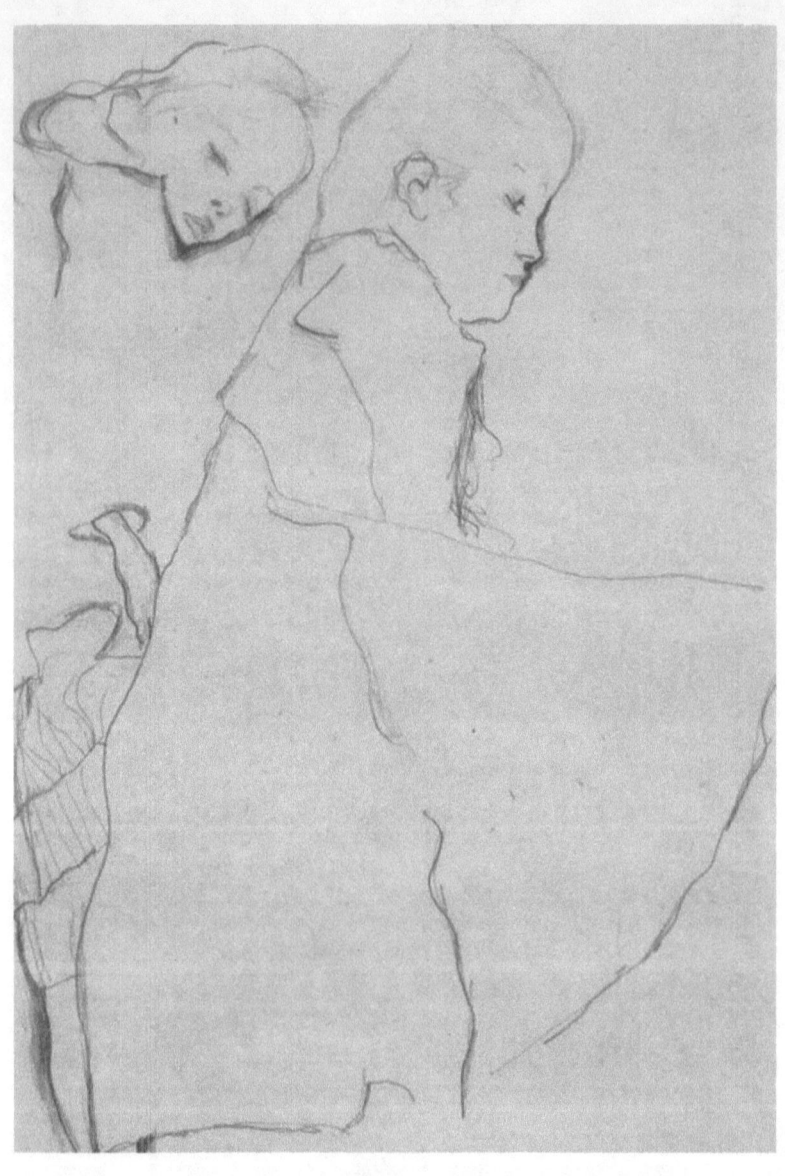

Two Sleeping Girls, 1911

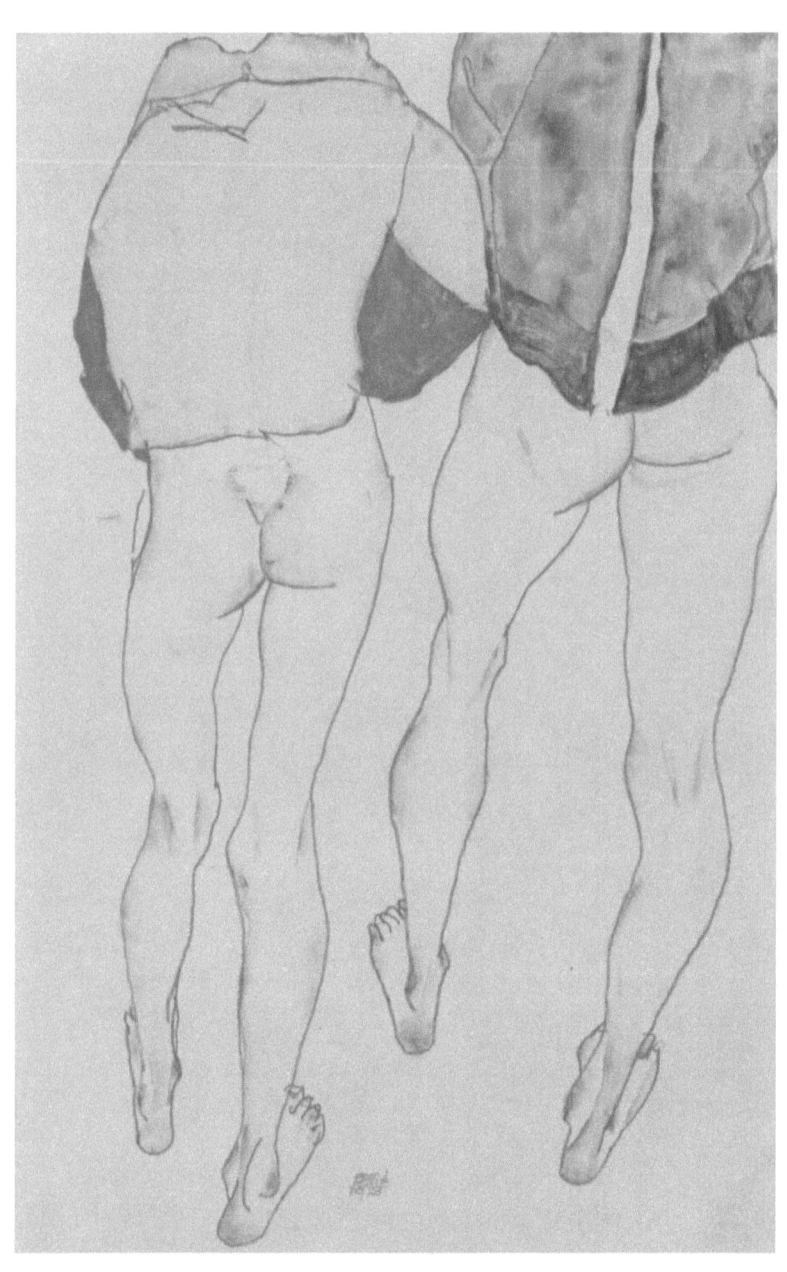

Two standing female nudes, 1913

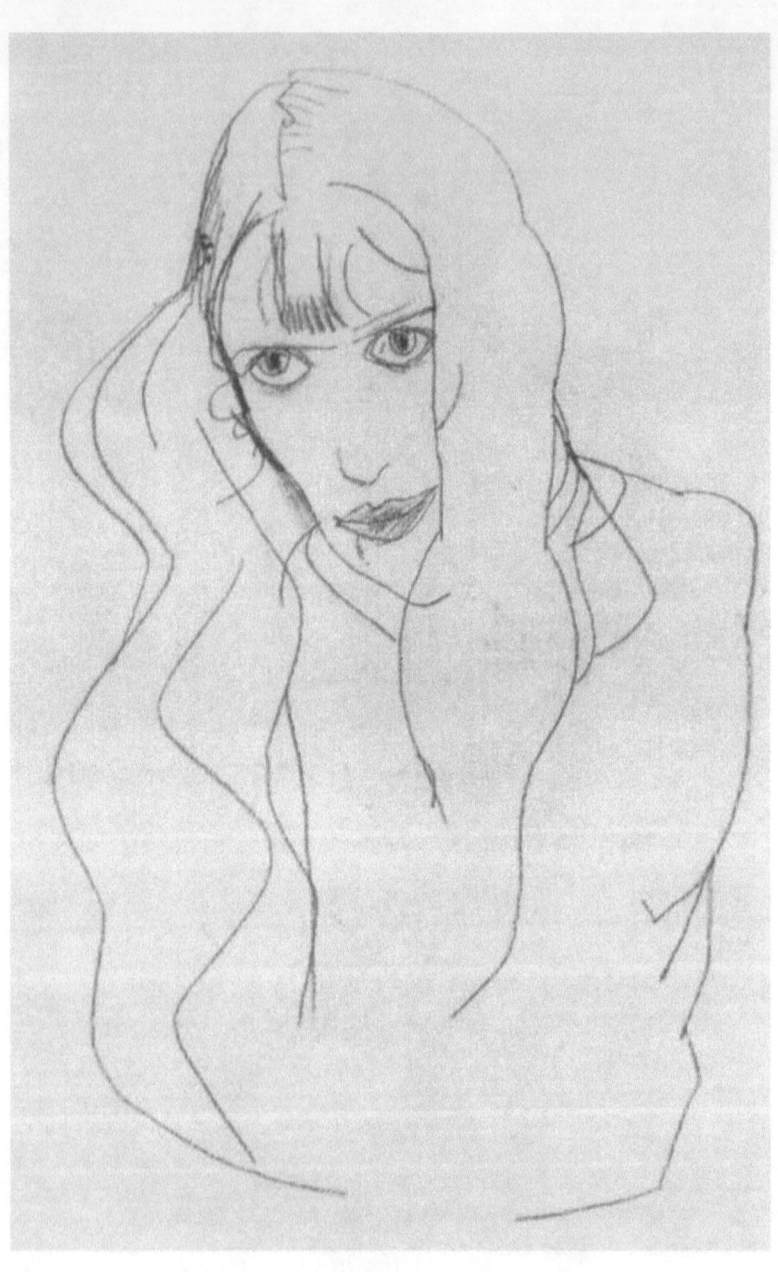

Women Portrait (Wally), 1913

www.ingramcontent.com/pod-product-compliance
Lightning Source LLC
Chambersburg PA
CBHW020913180526
45163CB00007B/2719